Peer
Counseling
in the Church

Peer Counseling in the Church

Paul M. Miller

Introduction by Wayne E. Oates

HERALD PRESS
Scottdale, Pennsylvania
Kitchener, Ontario
1978

Library of Congress Cataloging in Publication Data

Miller, Paul M.
　Peer counseling in the church.

　Bibliography: p.
　1. Peer counseling in the church. I. Title.
BV4409.M54　　259　　78-9299
ISBN 0-8361-1854-5

PEER COUNSELING IN THE CHURCH
Copyright ©1978 by Herald Press, Scottdale, Pa. 15683
　Published simultaneously in Canada by Herald Press,
　Kitchener, Ont. N2G 4M5
Library of Congress Catalog Card Number: 78-9299
International Standard Book Number: 0-8361-1854-5
Printed in the United States of America
Design: Alice B. Shetler

10 9 8 7 6 5 4 3 2 1

I dedicate this book to my grown children, sons and daughters, son-in-law and daughters-in-law, who give me so much good counsel about how to cope with problems I encounter in living. It's great to be a grandfather and to give and receive counsel from loved ones across the life-span.

I dedicate it also to ordinary Christians with the extraordinary concern to help other ordinary Christians cope with the problems they meet during life's ordinary days.

CONTENTS

Author's Preface — 9
Introduction by Wayne E. Oates — 11

Assumptions and Approach — 13

1 Attitudes and Skills Essential to Counseling — 17
2 Tactful Beginnings of the Counseling
    Relationship — 47
3 Skills in Responding and Intervening in
    Counseling — 73
4 Vocational Counseling — 107
5 Premarital Counseling — 121
6 Marriage Problem Counseling — 141

Concluding Thoughts — 159

Readings and References (Bibliography) — 163
The Author — 167

AUTHOR'S PREFACE

I have written this book to help the church train mature members to be helpful counselors to one another. Much literature is available for Sunday school classes and study groups to help members of congregations to be educators of one another. But almost nothing has appeared to help prepare ordinary church members to do peer counseling.

Pastors may want to use this book as part of their training program for those in the congregation who share in spiritual leadership, visitation, and calling upon members who are undergoing crises.

Sunday school classes, house fellowships, and growth groups may decide to study the book together, discussing the ideas first in pairs and then as a full group.

Several professional "helpers" who kindly read the manuscript of this book suggested that its ideas are so probing that any "helping Christian" could well read it as part of his or her private devotions.

I confidently expect that as the use of paraprofessionals continues to increase, as the human potential movement further removes the stigma from giving and receiving help with feelings, many churches will be ready to train their members in peer counseling.

Some congregations may want to "professionalize" the program by pretesting members who have shown a natural tact and desire to help people, and then training them to assist in the counseling ministries of the congregation. Because *Peer Counseling in the Church* frankly assumes the Christian perspective, it could be used along with other training manuals prepared by secular universities.

Paul M. Miller
Goshen, Indiana
December 13, 1977

INTRODUCTION

Paul M. Miller has taken the uniqueness of his own heritage as a Mennonite and the richness of his experience with behavioral sciences such as psychology, psychotherapy, and sociology and has blended them into a person-to-person conversation with the working member of a Christian community. His objective is not to write to "professionals," although his concepts are reliable ones from a technical point of view. Rather he speaks to church members and neighbors and reflects with them on how they can be genuine and realistic in their care of persons. *Peer Counseling in the Church* is an awareness-raising book for the lay person who will read it a chapter a week and spend the rest of the week implementing the new insights gained.

Russell Dicks used to say that 90 percent of the real help people receive comes from their friends, not through highly trained and paid professionals. The space age has taught us the crucial importance of life-support systems. We could not have put a person on the moon without elaborate life-support systems of food, oxygen, communication, and equipment. Neither can we keep a person on the earth, alive and well, without an excellent life-support system. That system is composed of warm, consistent, trustworthy, and sensible confidants among our friends—persons with whom we can be responsibly intimate and open. The peer-group counseling which Paul M. Miller advocates is aimed at developing that kind of life-support fellowship in the church.

Hopefully, the activation of such peer-group counseling in the church will soften and melt those barriers of respectability that keep people from sharing with each other their mutual woes and celebrations. Too often shame keeps us from sharing our joys and celebrations, except for the most obvious ones. The most obvious woe is a critical illness or a death. The most obvious occasion for celebration is the birth of a new baby. Beyond these, little is shared, except in most cases a wedding. Divorce, imprisonment, sudden poverty, marriage conflict, the battering of children or wives, the venality over a family estate are just a few examples of hurts that are normally dealt with in secret or outside the pale of the church. Paul M. Miller calls for making more use of the compassion and caring dimensions of the Christian faith by developing a "peer-counseling mood" among Christians.

I urge you to read this book meditatively both individually and in small groups. *Peer Counseling in the Church* is carefully written by a person of remarkable capacity to communicate with you in your own language and without a lot of fancy technicalities. You will be edified in the Spirit of Christ as you do so.

Wayne E. Oates, ThD
Professor of Psychiatry and Behavioral Sciences
Director, Program in Ethics and Pastoral Counseling
University of Louisville School of Medicine
Louisville, Kentucky

ASSUMPTIONS AND APPROACH

Counseling, as used in this book, is a series of interviews which one mature person holds with another one in an effort to assist that person to gain insight and to solve a problem. Counseling is a specialized and carefully structured form of friendship in which the total attention of both persons is focused upon the life of the one with an admitted problem. To be effective the counselor must possess mature attitudes, the capacity for sustained and perceptive listening, the skills of tactful intervention, all arising from a deep grasp of human nature. Counseling requires and assumes a wide range of interpersonal relationships. When the counselor is consciously seeking to serve from Christian motivations, some additional dynamics are added.

I will assume that many helping relationships of caring love are already going on, and that additional understandings and skills can upgrade many of them into Christian counseling. Twenty years of counseling within educational, medical, and mental health institutions have convinced me that too many people "go away for counseling" who could and should have recieved help in their home church. Just a few hours of total attention, of genuine caring, of listening love, of tactful suggestions, and of wise intervention would have met the need of the vast majority of those who left their congregations and paid hard cash to receive counseling elsewhere. By looking away from their fellow Christians and expecting to find help elsewhere, they lessened what their own congregation could do for them.

I will assume also that it is Christ's intention that Christians should meet a larger share of one another's needs than usually occurs. The Scriptures clearly assume that God's people are to bear one another's burdens. Only so do they fulfill the law of Christ. Christians are to rejoice with those who rejoice, weep with those who weep, and help one another probe the deeper meanings of the mountain peaks and valleys of life.

Christians should initiate counseling with one another. The scriptural view of the church implies the imperative for active caring, for initiating conversation about ultimate concerns, for actually going to the brother or sister whenever need or hurt is detected. "If your brother sins against you, go and tell him his fault, between you and him alone." "If a man is overtaken in any trespass, you who are spiritual should restore him in a spirit of gentleness. Look to yourself, lest you too be tempted." Christians are to counsel with one another about life's sorrows and tragedies. They are to weep with those who weep. They are to be involved caringly in both the normal developmental and the emergency crises of one another's lives. A helping situation is usually described as one in which a person approved as a helper-healer meets in structured fashion with a person explicity seeking help. All these conditions can be met in peer counseling.

In many churches which practice adult baptism and

which stress that membership implies the readiness to accept the responsibility for mutual decisions, the promise "to give counsel to the church and receive counsel from the church" has been central to the vow of baptism. In such churches, mutual counseling is imperative.

This book will assume that Christ, as head of His living body, the church, is intensely serious about life from Himself as the head flowing into every part of the body through the arteries of honest caring, frank counseling, and admonition. The caring and assistance in problem solving which goes on in a good family remains the model for the congregation's life. Apostles referred to the church as God's household. Christ promised that anyone who joins His movement will discover, in glad amazement, that he or she has fallen heir one hundredfold to fathers, mothers, brothers, and sisters. Counseling one another can help to make this happen.

From this point on I will not discuss counseling abstractly. I will not talk about counselors in general, or mature counselors, or tactful counselors. I will not talk about the counselor preparing himself (or herself), discipling himself, deploying himself as a helping person, and training himself to recognize resistances, to reflect back inconsistencies, to summarize gains, and the like. I will talk directly to you who would counsel. This will help me be personal about a helping skill which is very personal in its demands.

You who read this book will hear me as I intend to be heard if you keep applying the ideas and suggestions to yourself. Try to avoid distancing yourself by holding the ideas "out there" and surveying them as a theory about how "they" (other Christians) might do counseling.

Please assume as you read, that God's Spirit may be

calling you to be a Barnabas, "a son of consolation."
Maybe God wants to equip you to "put heart into" other
members of your congregation just when they need it.
He may be calling you to engage in loving confrontation
with your fellow Christians as they face themselves, one
another, and their God. Count it a privilege to help them
deal honestly with issues of doing justly, loving mercy,
seeking truth, restoring peace, maintaining integrity, and
deepening understanding.

1
ATTITUDES AND SKILLS ESSENTIAL TO COUNSELING

What are the attitudes and skills to cultivate if you wish to become a good counselor? A survey of the literature over a twenty-year period reveals that certain ones recur again and again. Combined they create a profile of a mature and well-rounded person.

When these attitudes and skills are merely tabulated, they create a long "shopping list" for you to seek. Beginning with "common sense," the lists urge that you as a counselor be openminded, mature, kind, tolerant, sympathetic, objective, tactful, intelligent, flexible, warm, and well trained. In addition you should actively come through as a good listener, a person who likes people, is able to handle pressures and anxiety without undue strain, uses humor appropriately, and is skilled in interpersonal relationships.

Since a list of two dozen attitudes and skills is unwieldy, I have grouped them in ten basic categories in this chapter.

1. *Develop Personal Warmth*

One of the first essentials, if you are to help another person as a counselor, is that you possess personal warmth. This quality is hard to define. Some persons seem to possess personal warmth without trying, but everyone can seek to grow in it.

You have "personal warmth" if other persons feel that you are aware of them, interested in them, and are easy to approach. They somehow sense that you are available. If they approach you they know they will be welcomed as a guest and that you will be a gracious host.

Your ready smile and welcoming glances help to convey warmth. But your smiles must be genuine, meant sincerely for the person. Smiles easily become phony if they are worn like makeup. Smiles almost drive people away if they are put on as part of sales appeal. A fixed smile worn by habit, or because you feel you are "on camera," will not be an asset in counseling. It detracts from sincerity.

Your warmth toward another human being grows out of your conviction that you and that person are alike in your depth. Because of God's image you both possess, you are extensions of one another's concreteness. A one-

ness between you already exists, waiting to be ac-
knowledged. You recognize this deep affinity with glad
awe and reverence. You both believe your individual
lives will be enriched by knowing one another.

Your warmth will be greater if you are honestly feeling
that somehow the counselee you seek to serve is also
necessary for your own growth as a person. Blessings can
flow both ways if you can enter a relationship of honesty
and depth.

Real warmth toward the one you attempt to counsel
requires that you recognize that this person is a once-for-
all and absolutely unique creation of God. This person is
so precious in God's sight that you would not want to
control or manipulate him, look down upon him, or
"play god" in his life.

If your welcoming warmth is real, the counselee will
sense that it does not matter at all to you whether he or
she is high or low on the social ladder, nor whether ethnic
or cultural ties between you already exist. If you understand just a bit of your own uniqueness, and are willing
to deploy your own unique self to help a loved one to
grow, you can also accept your counselees in their
uniqueness.

Your welcoming warmth must be something deeper
than charm. It must be more than mere charisma. It must
be more realistic than a superficial Pollyannaish optimism. Genuine warmth must be present, waiting to en-
circle and enfold the counselee. It must comfort and support the counselee. But warmth does not mean that you
must be a "nice guy," overly gentle, and sweet with
people. If you are self-confident, yet humble and genuine, you can be truly warm.

If you are not naturally a warm person, and yet you do

want to counsel a fellow Christian as need and opportunity arise, what can you do to increase your personal warmth? You can refresh your faith in the image of
God which He has given to every person. You can discipline yourself to avoid absentminded reveries while in
the presence of other persons. You can force your mind to
stop woolgathering and to return to attentiveness to
persons around you. You can start to invest yourself in
persons, and your caring and warmth will increase. You
can train yourself to notice how many persons seem
lonely and isolated and longing for warmth and caring.
You can evaluate how superficial the pleasantries are
which are passed off as conversation, even in a group
which desires to be Christian. You can respond to
warmth offered to you by others. You can pray for grace
to become a warmly caring person. These self-disciplines
can increase your capacity to give out honest warmth,
and this preceeds effective counseling.

Your warmth can have still deeper meaning if you
draw near to persons in crisis believing that this moment
may be for them a propitious moment—a time when
eternity is breaking in, a time when the living God is
confronting and calling them, a "burning bush" on the
backside of their own personal desert, an hour of decision
from which they can move forward with new power and
meaning. Your warmth will be felt as reverence for their
lives, for their life-and-death issues.

You will expect your counselee to talk honestly about
his emotions. It will help if you set the example with a
heartfelt and sincere regard for your counselee's worth as
a person. Communicate your emotional availability.
Model a good interpersonal relatedness in the way you
reach out toward your counselee. If you appear stiff, with

your body position pulled away from your counselee, you make it doubly hard for your counselee to like you, trust you, and to open up.

Your gestures should be sincere, your voice soft and firm, your smiles sincere, your face animated, your eye contact pleasant, your head sometimes nodding in assent, your rate of speech moderate, and your whole demeanor relaxed.

2. *Learn to Evoke and Inspire Trust*

You must be able to evoke trust on the part of other people if they are to come to you for counsel. They must somehow believe that you are trustworthy. They must feel that it would be safe for them to open to you the deep and even shameful secrets of their lives and that you are willing to face life with them.

In the world of law, health, banking, tax consulting, and diplomacy, people trust professionals to keep secrets. People will tell their tax consultant about their private financial affairs, their medical doctor about their bowel functioning, or their attorney about their plans to seek a divorce. People trust such professionals because they are professionals. They hang out their shingles and bind themselves to a code of ethics which includes trustworthiness in keeping secrets. The average citizen can be trusted to keep secrets and to decide fairly if called to serve on a jury. But can one trust a fellow Christian to serve as counselor? Many people aren't sure!

Ask yourself whether you have indeed established a well proven record of dependability in your community. If your neighbors had to list the ten most trustworthy persons in the community, would your name be on their list? There is no shortcut to building such trust.

But what if you destroyed or tarnished people's trust in you by a stupid fling some while ago? How can you regain trust if you have betrayed the confidence people once placed in you? These are painful but supremely important questions. There are a few things you can do to begin the slow process of rebuilding trust.

Make a clean break with anything in your past which tarnished people's trust in you. Make restitution for what you have done wrong. Determine to avoid any two-facedness or pretense in any area of your life. It's hard to radiate signals of absolute honesty in your life if you are secretly withholding the tithe in your giving, when your conscience keeps saying you should pay it. It's hard to come across as a completely honest and trustworthy person if you are all the while falsifying items in your tax reports. It's hard for people to trust you if they hear you gossip about others.

What can you do to become a person who, without a professional shingle to hang out, still evokes trust? You can go on establishing a record of proven performance. You can avoid unexplained or sudden shifts in your lifestyle. You can refuse to say anything behind people's backs which you would not be willing to say to their faces.

If you sincerely want to serve as a counselor to fellow Christians and to others who come to you for help, read up on human nature. Try to understand what makes people tick. Deliberately ventilate your own biases and narrow points of view brought along from your own childhood. Consciously work at becoming a trusting person and at modeling relationships of trust.

You can increase the trust others have in you if you practice searching out both sides of every issue. Slowly people come to believe that you are habitually fair to both sides or persons in any problem. You can deliberately stop and say, "But on the other hand . . ." and then ponder carefully what an honest opponent would have the right to say.

You can evoke trust if you practice the careful setting of limits. Set limits upon what you say. If you really know nothing about medicine, be careful not to comment. If you really know little about retardation, humbly admit this and gladly refer your counselee to someone more knowledgeable in this area.

You can evoke trust if you show that you care deeply about confidentiality. Carefully enter a covenant of confidentiality with the counselee which outlines under what conditions things shared between you dare to be repeated elsewhere.

If you have been faithful in your servant role, as a faithful friend in times of trouble, the giver of gifts of mutual aid, ready always to do the deed of lowly service whenever needed, then you will already be trusted as you begin to counsel. At other times you will have served in your prophetic role as teacher, exhorter, admonisher, and caller to repentance. This should help your counselees to trust you as a person of godly concern, courageous honesty, and deep compassion. Your role as counselor is quite different from your prophetic one, but need not clash if you are a flexible person capable of great breadth and depth, and if you know both roles well. If you are rigidly fixed in the prophetic model of relating, you cannot really be an effective counselor.

You can be so confident of your worthiness and acceptability before an all-knowing and holy God that you have nothing to hide from Him. This is the transparently honest and open life which relates freely to another human being with nothing to hide. As you live with your life open to inspection by°both God and fellowman, you expect other persons to like you. You actually feel that if persons only knew you better they would like you even more. This attitude inspires trust.

As you go on counseling with other persons, and prove that you can "sit where they sit" and can help them where they hurt, you gain trust and confidence in your own ability to help. Others trust you more as your own trust in yourself grows.

3. *Seek Accurateness in Empathy*

To be helpful as a counselor, you need to be able to detect how things are in the secret inner world of a counselee. You must not only be able to empathize, to pick up the "vibes," and to read the signals of what is going on inside the counselee's head and emotions, but you must empathize accurately. You must sense how much hope is mingled with how much despair and how much resistance to change is blended into the person's desire to change. While persons are halting between two opinions, you must be able to feel the strength of each opinion pretty much as the counselees are feeling them. You must seek to become almost at home in your counselee's inner world. You will need to rely upon your deepest intuitions and feelings and to slow down your mind's tendency to do rational diagnosis.

You can grow in your artistic skill of empathy if you learn to read body language. Notice how the person uses closeness and distance. Observe body posture and what it may be saying. Train yourself to read the counselee's tension signs such as drumming of fingers, wringing of hands, tapping of toes, or rocking back and forth. The way your counselee walks toward you, shakes hands, and is seated—all say something.

Deeper tensions are signaled by some people in a narrowing of the eyes, a tilt of the head, a shift in breathing rate, a licking of the lips, facial tics, or swallowing. Sometimes perspiration says, "I'm worried." Staring off into space has meaning. Avoiding eye contact does also. Nervous laughter is very revealing.

Train your ears to hear the infinite variety of meanings "between the lines" which people convey in their tones. Note the way they use pauses, humor, laughter, sarcasm, or questions. A break in a counselee's voice can be very revealing. By a kind of telepathy, or almost a thought transference, seek to feel what the counselee is feeling, understand what he or she is dreading, and sense what he or she is hoping. Lovers have always known that much more is going on between them than merely the words and visible actions. Similarly counselors know that much more is going on within the counselee than meets the eye or ear.

Pray all the while that God's all-knowing Spirit, which both you and your counselee share, will help you to hear the inner groanings which cannot be uttered. Pray for a meeting of meanings. Reflect back what you think your counselee is feeling so the counselee can correct you, and tell you if your empathy is still inaccurate.

What a deep and sacred joy it is for friend to commune with friend, for heart to beat with heart, for caring persons to sit and share joy or suffering in silence together. One of life's worst agonies is to believe that no one, absolutely no one, understands how you feel. Among life's sweetest joys is knowing that you are understood and accepted in your primordial depths, down where meanings and words come from, your innermost self usually known only by God.

Empathizing deeply with another person is good for the counselor's own mental health. Empathy lifts the counselor out of himself or herself, and has cathartic power. Just as observing great art or drama purges the soul of the observer so a deep empathizing with a counselee's inner drama has an enriching and cleansing effect upon the counselor. Don't strain or agonize to achieve empathy, or the over-effort may block it. Don't play any little games of deceit. Just be loving in the counselees' presence, with all your antennae out, as caringly sensitive as you can honestly be. Do not feel above your counselees, looking down upon them, but as an equal with them, meet them on the level, seeking to appreciate them as persons of great worth.

4. *Offer Unconditional Positive Regard*

The ability to go on loving another person unconditionally is a supreme credential and requirement for a counselor. To counsel those who are unlovely at times, you will need to be able to love the unlovely. Even if they turn against you, hate you, gossip about you, or seek to hurt you, you will need this unconditional positive regard.

Your counselees will need to be confident that nothing they can do or say will make you give them up or turn against them. In fact, the need to be held by a love that "simply will not let you go," this is one of the deepest and profoundest needs of every human being, whether children or adults.

What can you do if you really want to counsel others,

but you know that you tend to love persons who agree with your ethics and ideals, but to withdraw love from those who insult and violate what you hold dear? If there are certain needy persons for whom you simply feel revulsion, you should first admit this, in total honesty, to yourself, to God, and possibly to someone to whom you yourself go for counsel and help. One Christian nurse who attempted to respond in love to a male patient's request for counseling felt her love shifting to revulsion as he suddenly made passes at her, attempted to seduce her, and talked to her in revolting language. She herself found it necessary to seek counsel about how to cope with her problem.

Giving limitless love to needy counselees may come easier if you honestly remember how great a debt God has forgiven you. Remind yourself that in nearly every prayer you ask that you may receive forgiveness as you forgive others. When you see yourself afresh as a forgiven sinner before God, then you can handle feelings of revulsion toward the fellow sinners who are your counselees.

You can increase your ability to give unconditional positive regard if you remind yourself that God has already forgiven your counselees. God loved them all while they were yet sinners. Your counselees do not need to begin the process of change, of repentance, and of growth in order for God to love them. He loves sinners, while they are sinners. You are to be a laborer together with the forgiving God as your Counsel.

You can suspend your ordinary revulsions for shocking sin, much as nurses or doctors can overcome the revulsion they may have had at the sight of blood. As they keep looking beyond the necessary hurting and the temporary ugly mess which goes with surgery, so you as counselor can be saying honestly and in the depths of your spirit, "Neither do I condemn thee." You can honestly say this because you are also hoping for their future, "Go and sin no more."

As Jesus was able to look past the "Ugly Tax Gatherer," Zacchaeus, and see the true "Son of Abraham" beneath, so you as counselor can keep one eye fixed ahead upon what your needy and sinful counselees can become by God's grace. You can impute infinite worth to your counselees because of God's image within them, and remain optimistic because of your confidence in the power of God's grace.

But your limitless love must also be willing to let them go. Your counselees must know they are free to say no to you. Jesus insisted that, even while you are counseling your straying brother, you "let him be unto thee as an heathen man and a publican." Your counselees must know that you will go on loving them even if and while they go away from you.

You will sometimes need to warn your counselees lovingly about the "walls of reality" which there are in God's world. To help a young prodigal about to depart for some far country of riotous living to think about the possible result of his choice need not be seen as a withdrawal of love. Unconditional positive regard can be a very tough kind of love, a very honest kind of confrontation, and a very deliberate attempt to help your counselees to count the cost. Simply because your counseling attitude always must embody the limitless love of the gospel's good news does not mean that you withhold the law's firm reminder of the ruin your counselees face if they choose to refuse to respond to God's grace.

28

5. *Express Confidence in Your Counselee's Ability to Change*

Be confident in the counselee's power to decide and to grow. This is a crucial essential for your heart and mind as a counselor. You dare not accept a hyper-Calvinistic decree that some persons are not "elect" and are foreordained by God to be damned. You cannot accept an equally pessimistic Freudian view that man is essentially helpless in the grip of the all-powerful instincts of sex and aggression. You cannot accept even the counselees' own despair about themselves and their ability to repent and to begin again. For you, no case dare be labeled "hope_less."

You must somehow retain your faith that because of the image of God which is given to every human being, a tiny spot of "free space" is still preserved upon which oppressed and afflicted individuals can take their stand and can make their own free decision. Maintain your faith that God's loving providence is still in control, that God's image is still within man, that the last Adam's redemption is as far-reaching as the effect of Adam's fall, that God's loving Spirit is all pervasive and persistent, that God's people are still the chosen instrument of His redemptive activity, and that the ascended Christ is even now asserting his lordship and call. The Scriptures are still inspired and profitable. This counselee is still free to decide.

In this confidence you can help the counselee seek and find the remaining "free space" where a "yes" can be said. Even though a ghetto environment inculcated hate, a home taught deceit, horror movies modeled murder, life experience resulted in a feeling of futility, a gang lived by cynicism, and a "Watergate" brought more corruption, your counselees deformed by these influences can still hope. They can find the strength to respond to love in small steps leading upward and outward from their imprisoned existence. Some change can come in their own attitude which will ultimately make a vast difference. They can start to say "yes" to love and so to a new life.

— Because God already loves your counselee while yet a sinner, and because you are learning to do so, your counselee can gain "the courage of imperfection." Your counselee can feel the joy of beginning again. Sometimes you as counselor will find yourself believing in your counselees more deeply and profoundly than they can believe in themselves.

With a confidence grounded deeply in the heart of the Christian gospel that your counselee can really grow and change, you can then borrow ideas and methods from the responsibility therapy of a William Glasser. You can hold the counselee responsible to respond and to act decisively. You can borrow some rewarding-for-achievement methods from B. F. Skinner. You can work toward the satisfying of basic needs as suggested by Maslow and the humanists. You can help persons to individuate in fidelity to their own inner uniqueness as suggested by Carl Jung. You can challenge irrational thinking as suggested by the rational-emotive therapists such as Fritz Perls or Paul Hauck.

You can learn from the Transactional Analysis people how to recognize one's Parent, one's Adult, and one's Child speaking. This awareness might hasten adult maturity and self-control. You will try to avoid "putting down" parents as so many T. A. therapists inadvertently tend to do.

6. *Maintain an Inner Consistency*

You will need to be a congruent person if you are to be effective as a counselor. This means that you must maintain a core of inner consistency. You must be dependably the same no matter what role you are filling or playing. You dare not flit casually from one role to another as if life were a masquerade party.

Some teacher-preacher persons find incongruence in their inner selves between the person they are in the differing roles. When they are preaching, they see themselves as God's prophet, courageously proclaiming God's will for men. They assert, they declare, they affirm, and they stand unshaken for the absolutes of God's revelation, the triumphant certainties, and the "Thus saith the Lord." They point out God's holy and perfect will and plan for man.

In contrast, they feel like a different person altogether when they take up the priestly ministry of counseling. Then they see themselves as the forgiver, the supporter of the weak, the listener, the responder—accepting the best which failing man can bring before God. When counselees are pouring out the story of their failures, these teacher-counselors begin to wonder if they laid an impossible burden upon them when they proclaimed God's high and holy will. Such teacher-preachers need to get the problem solved first in their own inner life. What do they really believe about law and grace? Wherein lies their own personal courage or imperfection? Only then can their teaching-preaching enrich their counseling and their counseling enrich their teaching.

What can you do so that you are dependably the same person no matter what hat you are wearing or role you are filling? You need not be perfect before you dare counsel others, obviously, but you should be on your way. You should be working steadily to correct incongruent aspects of your own life.

Work toward congruence, toward inner cohesion and integrity as a person. Keep asking questions of yourself such as the following: Have I found my task in life so that I can feel "for this cause was I born, this one thing I do"? An all-engrossing task can become a focus around which you gather your own roots and heritage, your present choices and direction of growth, and your goal for your future.

Invite others to help discern your gifts and then affirm you in your ministry through these gifts. Bobbie Burns said poetically—

> O wod some power the giftie gie us,
> to see ourselves as ithers see us;
> It would from many a blunder free us
> and foolish notion.

Ask caring and spiritually discerning persons to give you feedback. They can see incongruities in your life better than you can. They can help you to get it all together. Try maintaining a "growth list" of personal goals.

Begin learning how to do "confessional meditation" as one aid toward achieving congruence. Keep a continuing record of your nighttime dreams and see how they align with your daydreams and visions of your future. Keep a journal of your inner life and reread it periodically. Share periodically in retreats and seminars which scrutinize the inner life and help one toward wholeness.

Seek to be a receiver of counsel as well as a giver of counsel. As you yourself go for counsel ask your counselor to help you evaluate the methods you are using to cope with life's hard places or life's difficult persons. Tell your counselor about times you are able to catch yourself at making excuses or rationalizing. Carefully evaluate the distancing devices you are using to cope with difficult persons. Invite your counselor to probe into the way you are handling your competitive drives and status hungers.

As you learn from your own life's sufferings, as you accept counseling about your problems and become more aware of your own functioning, you will be able to identify incongruous parts of your life and attempt to work toward wholeness. A careful listing of both your basic assets and your recurring mistakes may be revealing. Thoughtful reflection about the way your love and work habits have changed over the years may help you toward greater congruity.

7. *Grow in Personal Emotional Maturity*

Personal emotional maturity should be your goal even if you had no desire or intention to serve as a counselor to others. But counseling does test your emotional maturity, and so it becomes doubly important for a counselor. It is true that in groups like Alcoholics Anonymous and other lay helping groups some very immature persons are helping one another. But there is always the danger of "the blind leading the blind" unless the counselor possesses considerable emotional maturity as a person.

What ideal or goal can define emotional personal maturity? For you as a Christian counselor, "personal" tends to mean Christlikeness. What Jesus was and said and did constitutes your goal for mature personhood. You are seeking to grow in the measure of the stature of the fullness of Christ.

Maturity tends to mean for you the "grown-up" set of attitudes and characteristics which Jesus demonstrated. It is true always that you must admit, "I am not yet mature and I am not perfect, but I am following after what I see in Jesus." With this attitude you should be able to admit remaining needs in your own life without despairing, and to observe needs in your counselees' lives without despising or judging them as the ancient Pharisees did.

A part of the maturity you need is a realistic quest for perfection. An honest recognition that "I have not yet attained" will motivate you in your search for growth. You should be able to answer at once with specifics when someone asks you, "What are your goals for growth right now?" If you really want to move toward becoming professional in your understanding of human feelings, then you should arrange for some insightful and concerned person to ask you such probing questions at least once each year.

To balance this you need a deep sense of "okayness" before both God and man. If you have this you can both give and receive feedback and criticism without rejection coming through at a deep, subverbal level. You should be able to accept persons who differ from you without feeling a wordless urge to remake them.

An emotionally mature person is able to hold deep convictions without becoming dogmatic. You need to stake your whole future upon realities you trust, and yet remain open to new truths along life's way. Remain open to new truths about all that it means to follow Jesus from day to day, yet maintain the quiet certainty that Jesus will not be replaced or superceded as Savior and Lord in your life.

Because counseling so often moves slowly and visible results take time, you will need to be mature in the matter of patience. Don't pressure your counselees for immediate change. Developing insights which change convictions and eventually lives takes time. To become a good counselor you will need to be able to forgo immediate satisfactions for the sake of long-term goals. Society offers many instant foods, instant drinks, instant amusements. Some forms of religion offer magical and quick formulae for change. But Christian counseling takes patience. Often you can see only a small sprout, then a slowly growing stalk, and you wait quite a while to see the "full corn on the ear" of desired change.

As counselor you will need to be mature about disappointments and setbacks. Some counselees seem to take three steps forward only to take two backward. Counselees are free to quit any time and quite a few are not willing to endure the death which often precedes a resurrection or the pain which precedes the birth of a new hope.

To keep going in counseling you will need to be able to plug along without constant praise or thanks. Peer counseling does not pay well, either in cash or thanks or highly visible results. You will do your work in secret and few will reward you openly.

Among the other items which should remain on your own agenda for growth are the capacity both to give and to receive love from either males or females, the ability to feel and express gratitude sincerely, to sustain deep interpersonal relationships with widely diverse persons, to feel comfortable with individuals across the life-span, and to relate deeply with people of differing ethnic backgrounds.

Before you counsel others it is important to be keenly aware of your level of maturity-immaturity in the matter of exercising authority over other persons. This must be done without restricting their essential freedom, all the while submitting to the authority of others in a kind of radical subordination. The constant status battles, power struggles, efforts to be "one up" on one another or "one down" on one another are part of every counselee's problem. There is something seductive in being regarded as the all-wise guru, the great helper, the god-figure. This kind of power-over-others can corrupt a person totally.

Emotional maturity requires that you be comfortable about the full range of your own emotions—the agony and the ecstasy, the angers and the loves, the tears and the laughter, the fantasies and the fears, the emotions that go along with birth and death, the feelings that belong to baptism and funeral, to marriage and divorce, to promotion and retirement, to graduation and amputation, to career choice and cancer diagnosis, to the numinous and the breakdown. Human feelings span an awesome range, and you who would empathize with a suffering person must increase your emotional breadth and depth.

When you walk with persons through their peak and their passion experiences, their mountaintops and their valley of the shadow of death, you must beware lest the seams of your own soul be opened by the strain or lest you harden and insulate yourself and so become a cold professional.

Failure to continue endlessly dealing with personal immaturities may be one reason the suicide and divorce rate is so high among psychiatrists and therapists, and why

36

pastors come through as poorly as they sometimes do during psychodrama. (Psychodrama is a specialized form of role playing used primarily in group therapy.)

How can you increase your self-understanding? You can try, with absolute candor, to answer some soul-searching questions of self-analysis. Put down the first honest response you feel like making to "I am known as the kind of person who. . . ." Consider your answer in light of your goals for growth.

You can prepare a religious history of yourself and share the results with a group honest enough to give you feedback. Ask them to reflect back bias and distortion you should be aware of.

You can engage in reverent fantasy around your own idealized self-image. What do you really hope to act like and look like ten years from now? Take an emotional maturity test and ponder your five lowest scores. Dream a while of the person you hope to become in each area. Write down your answer to, "By God's grace and my gumption, I resolve to reach these five goals in my personal maturity—" Then see whether you can hold yourself to these goals as rigorously as a good coach holds an athlete to his agreed upon discipline.

You may find that writing and sharing a personal journal will help you to grow toward emotional maturity. Sharing your journal with a trusted and caring friend can double the value you gain through this discipline. Following is a list of twenty "probes" to guide you in your journal writing:

Twenty Personal Journal-Disclosures
Instructions

In your personal journal, write out your most carefully

considered answer to each of the following twenty "probes." Do one each day for twenty successive days, devoting twenty minutes to each one.

Then by mutual agreement with a peer you respect highly (such as your marriage partner), share your journal statement with one another. Invite feedback on what each of your honest self-disclosures reveals to the other person.

1. My parents praised me for _____, my parents scolded me for _____, and my parents made me feel that I was _____. If I could tell this all to them now, I would want them to omit discussing _____ above.

2. As I look back now, I feel my childhood environment was rich in _____, but I feel impoverished and somehow cheated in the following areas _____.

3. The most humiliating experiences I remember from my childhood are _____, from my adolescent years are _____, and from my adult years are _____.

4. While growing up, I was different from my siblings and peers in the following ways _____.

5. When I was a child, my fantasy-goal for my future was _____, as an adolescent it was _____, and now it is _____.

6. Of all the responsibilities I have carried in life, the most rewarding was _____, and most distasteful was _____.

7. The "boundary situations" of my life, when I faced myself, my Creator, and my destiny with the most earnestness were _____.

8. When I choose clothing for myself, I want to express the following things about myself _____.

9. When I am asked to discuss how I cope with my sexuality, I find it hardest to think through and say how I feel about the following areas _____.

10. Among the priorities of my life I rate the church as _____. I do this because _____.

11. The kind of persons I feel uncomfortable with, or with whom I would not want to work closely are _____.

12. If my house was aflame, and I could salvage only three possessions, I would save _____ and _____

and _____. They are most precious to me because
_____.

13. I feel I have an honest, I-Thou, intimate relationship in which I am known as I really am with the following persons _____. I select these persons for intimate sharing because _____.

14. I express my needs for privacy and solitude by _____.

15. At present I have made irrevocable commitments to _____. In the future I plan to commit myself more deeply to _____.

16. During my childhood I thought of God as _____, in adolescence I thought of God as _____, and now I think of God as _____.

17. The most intense sufferings I have experienced in my life were when _____. From these experiences I learned _____.

18. When I am near a dying person I feel _____. As I think seriously about my own certain death I _____.

19. If I were to write an obituary, describing the contribution my life has made, I would say that _____.

20. The hardest of the previous exercises for me to write about were _____. I think this was because _____.

8. Practice Appropriate Self-Disclosure

Appropriate self-disclosure is important in counseling. All persons are basically alike in their depth. Every deep need a counselee confesses will awaken some tremor in your own unconscious. Every problem revealed is one you have either worked through, are now working through, or puzzles you as you ponder how you would cope with it in your own life.

If you are able to keep admitting your own common humanity, and are humble enough to admit the partialness of your own maturity, the next question becomes, "How much self-disclosure would be most helpful to this counselee, at work on this problem, at this point in solving it?" Many counselors and therapists with long and successful experience would say, "Absolutely none!"

There may be some counseling situations when no self-disclosure is the most helpful to the counselee. It is conceivable that a few postvictorian matrons trying to recall sexy dreams to recite to an analyst will be helped if the counselor sits behind the couch impassively, remaining completely unknown as a person, almost invisible, and hides behind a pipe and a poker-faced expression. But the classic analyst model has very little application to counseling between brothers and sisters in Christ, where mutual openness is the ideal, and shared responsibility the goal. In fact, it may well be that the analyst model has been a great hindrance to a truly "churchly" model of counseling.

There will be times when you withhold for the moment some of what you are feeling or perceiving. Christ's attitude seems appropriate when He said, "I have yet many things to say to you, but you cannot bear them now" (John 16:12). Look for readiness, for levels of stress and anxiety, for teachable moments, and focus upon what will benefit the counselees. You need not comment upon your own counseling methods or style.

Although you are ready and willing for self-disclosure, and to share your own similar experience with the counselee, it may not be appropriate. This is the counselee's hour. The total attention of both yourself and counselee are focused upon his problem. Anything which might distract is excluded. It is not just an occasion of good fellowship, sharing, and conversation. On such occasions both should share. "You tell one and I'll tell one," is the rule. But in counseling you must hold your own problems in abeyance and discipline your impulses to talk too much. Share only if you are convinced your comments will help solve the counselee's present problem and not distract the attention and diffuse the focus. Your counseling should be quite different from the chitchat and usual give-and-take of informal friendly conversation.

Put your own problems on hold for a while and lay aside your intense search for their solution. Resist the temptation to judge or compare your counselee's maturity with your own. Suspend operations on all the other issues of your life so that, for the moment, you can serve your counselee. Counseling practically stops the instant you focus on your own needs rather than those of your counselee.

It may even be heartless and cruel at times for you to offer inappropriate self-disclosure. Reciting a success story from your own life may discourage and crush the counselee who cannot yet succeed at all in that given area. If, in an ill-advised attempt to show your common humanity and empathy, you share a contemporary failure in your own life in the same problem area in which the counselee is seeking help, the result may be discouragement and a feeling of two helpless people floundering in the mud together. You may refer the counselee to another counselor if your need in the same area is too acute at present. But counselees should not be asked to bear a double burden of trouble, both their own and yours.

It may be cruel for you to recite your own experiences in surgery when counseling a person who has just experienced an amputation. It is heartless for you, who have lost your fingers, to use that fact of self-disclosure in an attempt to comfort a person whose second leg is being amputated at the hip because of complications resulting from diabetes. (I was in this situation while serving as a hospital chaplain ten years ago. The amputee left the hospital never knowing that I had lost the fingers on one hand.)

Constantly remind yourself that the self-disclosure which is essential in open Christian fellowship must be restricted out of love for the counselee when a formal counseling situation has been agreed upon. Both you and your counselee must understand that while counseling is real friendship and fellowship, it is a very specialized form of caring and friendship. Specialized practices, special limitations, and appropriate disciplines must be followed. Your tactful use of self-disclosure is one such discipline.

There is reason to believe that when you disclose a carefully chosen and small portion of your own past experience, some part of your own present anxiety, some reality of your own present faith, or some aspect of your own hoped for future—and do so appropriately, skillfully, tactfully, caringly, wisely, and honestly—it often becomes a crucial and positive turning point in the counselee's own problem-solving and growth.

9. *Take Some Training in Counseling*

To become a teacher one expects to participate in a teacher's training program. Even more training is necessary to serve people through dental, eye care, or health care. Why should you not be willing to undergo some training if you wish to serve persons as counselor? Even though your natural warmth and common sense will go a long way toward making you an effective counselor, you are unwise to rely only upon them.

How can you, as a lay person, secure some training for your work as counselor? You can work toward achieving the attitudes and maturities listed thus far in this book. By covenanting with a friend to share problems and progress you can achieve much through self-discipline.

In addition, you can offer yourself as an interne to assist your pastor or any other trained person in the congregation. You can arouse interest in the congregation until a peer group of up to six persons covenants to work together in counseling. A good supervisor will assign a program of parallel reading. He will guide you as you take turns reporting to one another your work with case studies. The way to learn counseling is by actually doing counseling under constant and sustained supervision.

Increasingly, wide-awake congregations offer in-service training in counseling for their deacons, elders, and other elected leaders. You can ask to be part of such a program, even though you are not now an elected leader. Counseling is such a serious and important work that it is worth preparing yourself to do it well.

If the course is offered within driving distance, you may decide to take a quarter (12 weeks full time, or 30 weeks two days per week) of Clinical Pastoral Education. This is one of the finest training programs available, often strongly related to churchly realities. In some such programs serious attention is given to the integration of the learnings from "the living human document" (the person in crisis) with corresponding learnings from the documents of Scripture, hymn, and creed.

10. *Be as Professional as Possible*

Do not let your immediate reactions against mere

43

"professionalism" keep you from trying to be as professional as you can be. In our overly institutionalized society, in which almost every helping relationship has its price, you have a right to abhor "professionalism." The grapevine of common gossip sees this as "being careful to do only what you are paid to do." It follows that you should never help to fix your widowed neighbor's house unless your union contract allows for it and you perform within their professional restrictions. To many people professionalism suggests a narrow specialization, an unawareness of the whole person in his or her total needs.

Professionalism has also come to mean that you should not practice your specialty if you are engaged in something else at the moment. For example, a medical doctor may ignore his fellow golfer's injury unless he checks in at the office. The pastor who refuses to converse with a fellow golfer about guilt unless he checks in at the study may find his counterpart in the priest and the Levite who could not help the battered man on the road to Jericho.

You can avoid the snobbery which professionalism implies. You are free from the reputation of secular therapists who offer "forgiveness for guilt" and "an hour's worth of love for $35.00 to those wealthy enough to afford it." When thinking of a professional lawyer, professionalism suggests being authoritarian, power-oriented, and directive. The mythology of the medical professional includes wealth, prestige, and a conservative, scientific outlook. Fortunately when you counsel as one church member with another you escape the stigma of professionalism.

But you can be professional in the best sense of the word. Fortify yourself with some basic necessary information. Discipline yourself in some basic skills so that persons can trust your services to help them and not to harm them. Decide why you do or do not do a certain act in counseling by referring to basic principles you have learned. Don't allow yourself to be seen as a practitioner with a "bag of tricks." Neither should you present yourself as a "spiritual guru" with special wisdom because you have a lot of charisma. Primitive cultures reverence their charismatic "diviners" as all-wise counselors, but in the West you need other credentials.

Be professional in that you possess a quiet confidence in what you have to offer. You are fully aware of the time and energy required to do a thorough job of counseling and are prepared to give it. You are able to speak clearly about the things essential to counseling. You gladly hold yourself to standards of ethics, of information, and performance higher than many in society would require.

If you are concerned about the grouping of attitudes and skills which are essential to good counseling, if you are ready to put good theory and theology into actual practice, if you gladly adhere to accepted standards of good counseling procedure, and if you are aware of other helping resources in the community, then you have some of the qualities, skills, and proven performance which make you a professional, in the best sense of the word. You should be able to match your counselee's anxiety and uncertainty with your own self-confidence and composure.

2

TACTFUL BEGINNINGS OF THE COUNSELING RELATIONSHIP

1. *Make Yourself Available*

Making yourself available, is the first step into the counseling relationship and process. Professional counselors hang out their shingles, circulate brochures, or in other ways advertise their services and invite counselees to come.

These brochures and advertisements play on slogans like, "Your problem is more respectable than you think," "It's smart to see your analyst," "Get help the modern way," "It's not necessary for you to go on in distress," "Neurotics are superior people," "I've had a lot of cases like yours," "You are unique," "We reinforce your common sense," or "We are here to help you cope."

None of these sales pitches is appropriate when congregational members offer to counsel one another. Among God's people any concerned member may take the initiative. If you know that a solemn or happy crisis has come into a fellow member's life, you are almost dutybound to go. The Bible says, "<u>Rejoice with those who rejoice, weep with those who weep" (Romans 12:15).</u> The Apostle Paul advises that if anyone is overtaken with a fault, ye who are spiritual should go in the spirit of meekness, seeking to restore, considering yourselves lest you also be tempted (Galatians 6:1). And Matthew 18:15 says, "If your brother sins against you, go and tell him his fault, between you and him alone. If he listens to you, you have gained your brother." As my father used to say, "If you see your brother has need, do not hold back your caring and compassion from him."

The duty and the right to initiate counseling is a great strength for you. Almost all other counselors, psychiatrists, clinical psychologists, family counselors, attorneys, and the like must wait until the counselee comes to ask for counsel. Persons usually wait until they are desperate before they do so. Often irreparable damage has been done to themselves and others by that time. In contrast, Christians who offer counseling to one another can do preventative counseling, heading off much suffering by innocent bystanders and children. You capitalize on a loving fellowship of mutual caring for each other. You can rely upon a readymade support group in the congregation for ongoing, post-counseling care. Congregational counseling is superior to professional counseling in some other important ways.

When you offer your Christian concern through counseling, you are not suggesting that your counselees are "patients," and that you will "treat" them. The suggestion of sickness and of passivity in those terms you will be glad to avoid. Some counseling centers insist that the patient "discuss with your therapist if you wish to contact your clergyman." In contrast with this, you assume that your counselees are in continuing contact with the pastor.

In making yourself available, you will want to be sure that you do not initiate counseling of an intensive kind while the person is in intensive counseling program with the pastor, or with a therapist of the area. One counseling of a depth nature is enough at one time. Offer to stand by in a warmly supportive friendship and fellowship if you discover a fellow member is in the midst of an intensive counseling process.

You make yourself available by using the counselee's language and terminology, even slang that is personally meaningful to the counselee. But don't carry this too far. Keep holding yourself available even though your counselee continues to discuss fairly neutral and "safe" material for a while. The relationship between you must be well established before your counselee will feel secure enough to share deeply sensitive material.

2. *Rejoice with the Person's Rejoicing*

One tactful beginning for counseling a fellow Christian can be made during frustration points of engaging in congregational services together. Attempts to cooperate in congregational committees, choirs, and projects bring close interaction. Needs are often laid bare along the way. Tempers explode. Frustrations are vented. Heavy loads of anxiety brought along from family or job may surge to the surface. Outbursts of tears, repeated sighs, moods of depression may be unverbalized cries for help. As a Christian who is willing to counsel, offer a listening ear. "Hey, I can see you are hurting. Would you like to tell me about it?" "Boy, that must be heavy. I'd be willing to take time with you to try to understand, at least so I can remember you in prayer more realistically." "How would you like to get together so you can tell me about it?" "Let me take you out to lunch, or find a quiet place to talk while we have a cup of coffee."

You can offer to counsel with a fellow Christian also during happy crises or meaningful milestones of the fellow Christian's life. "You know, I'm glad you're going to be baptized next Sunday." "I'd like to hear what the experience is meaning to you. Could we find time when you could share with me about it?"

If you yourself see the deep significance of this happy crisis, a whole cluster of concerns force their way to the surface. What should a vow to be faithful to Christ and His church, even unto death, mean to the counselee? What can one do if the whole service, from which a "peak experience" had been anticipated, should go "blah"? When you say that baptism is the "answer of a good conscience to God," just what do you mean? How can the significance of the special occasion be lived out during ordinary days? This counseling session may take a format more like a traditional interview. But the counselees may reach out for help in a specific area and you can set a contract for further sessions in counseling.

You can make an offer to rejoice with a fellow Christian in connection with any one of the high points along life's pilgrimage. High school graduation time can be a good time to pause, in guided retrospect, and think upon the meaning of this "puberty ritual" of our culture. It can become a time to ask how well learnings are being integrated with a "childhood" faith brought along from earlier years. How does your counselee leave behind the characteristics of "childishness" in religion, such as the self-centered, the irresponsible, the dependent, the sulking, the impetuous, and the gullible? Does your counselee experience a basic repentance from these "childish" ways so as to move on to a "childlike faith" during adult life? A "childlike faith" during adult life may help an adult to be spontaneous, inquisitive, trusting of self and others, with little need to compete or to win, but to be deeply alive and aware of all that is going on here and now. Jesus warned that it is not easy for an adult to enter the kingdom like a child and to become childlike. "Except you repent, you can't do it," He said.

An engagement announcement can become for you an occasion to rejoice with a fellow Christian. An infinite variety of matters of supreme importance deserve attention. How do your counselees know a lifetime love from a deep friendship? How can they be sure that two persons who are compatible at this stage of their growth will not slowly grow apart if both develop in fidelity to their own still-latent uniqueness?

Check with the pastor before you contract with an engaged couple for a sustained series of premarital counseling sessions. Increasingly pastors are inviting qualified lay persons to assist them in this very enjoyable counseling ministry.

If you have learned how to move alongside a fellow

51

Christian at times of baptism, engagement, and graduation, you will discover that they are only illustrations of
many more such occasions for counseling. You can
counsel around the happy occasion of marriage, of wedding anniversaries, of vocational choice, of a job promotion, of childbirth, of vocational change, of retirement, of
claiming elder-statesman status, of publishing a book, of
a housewarming, of writing a song, of finishing a quilt, of
recommitment to Christ, of speaking in tongues, of
experiencing healing, of narrow escape from tragedy, of
experiencing providential leadings or answers to prayer.
As a counselor you know that such experiences call for
sharing with introspection, reflection, praise to God, and
maybe counseling. Any of these may become, for the
counselee, a "burning bush," a spot of "holy ground"
where the living God calls and confronts anew. Such
happy milestones provide excellent opportunities for
interaction at a meaningful level in contrast to the many
superficial encounters in our modern world.

As a counselor you can offer yourself to be available.
You can begin with, "As we were talking about your
experience, I noticed you were having mingled and deep
feelings and concerns at one point. Would you like to
share about those?"

3. *Weep with the Person's Weeping*

You can move to the side of the person who is hurting
and offer your caring and listening love. Resist the im-
pulse to pass by on the other side when someone is suffering. Open your heart of compassion to the person
stricken by tragedy or loss. Many persons seek for
counsel when they must walk through some valley of the
shadow. But you do not need to wait until they get

desperate enough to come. You can go to their side.

Establishing rapport may involve just sitting in silence a while. Preparation for counseling may call for you simply to be caringly there. Do not rebuke their tears, nor try to get them to talk before they are ready. Do not treat them as if they should be ready at once to engage in an unemotional, logical conversation. You need not respond to every outburst of anger. If you do not know what to say, admit this and just weep with the weeping person for a while. Do not offer your counseling as a mysterious or magical event.

In counseling with persons who are undergoing a hurtful crisis, begin by ministering through very simple deeds of love. Make sure they are getting the medical attention they need. Help to rally the supporting resources of the congregation and family around them. Wait for the counselee's readiness before you try to proceed with the actual counseling process. Emotional first-aid usually must precede counseling.

The hurting experiences which might call for your counseling approach can include "acts of God" like storms, floods, lightning, fires, drought, or epidemic. You will face additional problems in the minds of your counselees when innocents are suffering, or if they themselves are suffering as a result of something about which they had no choice. You can expect anger and guilt to be mingled with their other feelings.

If you are ready to counsel as you weep with those who weep, you will want to be sensitive to times of sickness, of terminal illness, and of death. Be alert to amputations, to the parents' needs when a deformed child is born, to the occasion when mental illness strikes a family.

You may be led to weep with those who weep more

silently and secretly when a son or daughter has been suspended from school, gotten into drugs, rebelled, entered an ill-advised marriage, become addicted to drink or to drugs, or in some other way has disappointed or humiliated the parents.

You may need to detect the secret sorrows when love is growing cold in marriage, children are failing in school, debts are mounting, in-laws are clashing, unemployment is hurting, or a church split is dividing friends. Your tact will be supremely tested when you attempt to counsel persons on a sorrow or a shame which they very much want to keep secret.

The list of human need to which you can respond as counselor is almost endless. The child overshadowed by a brilliant older brother or sister could profit by understanding counseling. The man forced to retire at sixty-five could use help. The aged person lonely in a convalescent home should receive your counsel. The shut-in facing a slow recovery, the couple hurting from a broken engagement, the single person longing for fellowship, the widow forced to sell her home, the homosexual ashamed about his sexuality—all these need the listening love, the understanding response, the supportive word, and the problem-solving help which you can give if you are a tactful counselor.

Christ said we are like children playing at life in their little games in the marketplace if we are afraid to rejoice with one another's peak experiences and to weep with one another in the "valley of the shadow of death" experiences. "We piped to you, and you did not dance; we wailed, and you did not mourn" (Matthew 11:17). People afraid of both weddings and funerals, of both ecstasies and agonies, who want only life's safe plateaus, miss the grandeur and misery of man. They are apt also to miss the greatness and grace of God!

The average full-time counselor has a client load of 26 (a 26-member congregation), all needing to be wept with! As peer counselor in the congregation you can have both kinds of sharing. You get to share in the joys of your counselees too.

4. *Establish Rapport During the First Interview*

Going about establishing rapport will need to be handled differently if you have initiated the session than if the counselee did so. If you initiated the session, you will likely need to continue taking the initiative, at least until the counselee feels urgency enough to seize the initiative.

To help establish rapport make the counselee comfortable, treat the person as your honored guest, take steps to insure privacy and guarantee that you will not be interrupted. Your own home, or your counselee's, or a room at the church may meet these requirements.

If the counselee seems to want to engage in small talk, you should go along with this for a while. The person may be testing the waters before plunging in. Small talk can help to clarify the background of the problem and help you and the counselee to become comfortable with one another. You do not need to explain your counseling style to your counselee. Just employ it consistently and he or she will sense it.

Should you just plunge in at any point the counselee prefers, or should you ask for a rather systematic coverage, beginning with the history of the problem (and often incidentally of the person), its present symptoms, and what the counselee has already tried? Experienced counselors keep flexible to do it either way. Usually if you begin with the present problem, and gradually draw out the various angles and dynamics of it, you will accumulate most of what you need to know to upgrade the counselee's problem-solving ability. All the while, be careful never to regard the counselee as sick, although he or she may be discouraged, perplexed, angry, or crying out for help. Regard the counselee always as a chooser, a selector of values, a decision maker, and searcher for meaning. Never think of the counselee as your patient, or your client, nor of yourself as his doctor or his lawyer.

What can you say when a counselee apologizes profusely for having a problem, or for bothering you? You can try to hear the counselee's meanings. The counselee may be meaning, "Good people don't have problems." If this seems to be the case, you can respond with what your honest attitude is about this. Some counselors reassure with a reply such as, "In a world as twisted as ours the very best people are bound to have problems adjusting to it." This may be too abstract for some.

If the counselee is finding it hard to begin, sit at a ninety-degree angle, with a small table or piece of furniture nearby. Thus, if the counselee is not yet comfortable in looking you in the eyes, the person can look straight ahead without you getting in the way. Then the counselee can face you when he or she feels ready to do so. It is usually best to sit rather close, so you can read body language better and convey warmth and caring.

Be aware of your own feelings all the while, as well as to those of the counselee. If a flush of impatience or dislike rises within you, deal with it by sheer power of your will and mind. If you bring to bear your lifelong commitment and faith, momentary impulses can be overcome. Keep in firm charge of your inner thoughts throughout the interview. Delay any confrontation until your relationship is deep and strong.

What if your mind actually wanders and you miss an important statement? It is better to admit it frankly and ask the person to repeat than to go on knowing you have missed an important piece of what the individual was willing to share.

If your counselee plops a vast, complex, and seemingly hopeless problem into your lap, and then seems to sit back with a sigh as if to say, "There it is; now you solve it," disclaim omnipotence at once. "I sense that you do have a real problem, and I don't have an immediate solution. But I'm ready to join you and to assist you as we begin a serious search into the sources and possible solutions to your problem."

As your counselee reduces his or her vague feelings and problems to words, keep in mind that this in itself begins to give a sense of control over the problem. Sometimes just asking a counselee to tell you what he or she hates and loves can start the process of honest search going. If your counselee feels ashamed and inadequate, ask the person to list past accomplishments, as if you needed them for background data. This review sometimes gives the counselee courage to plunge into the current problem.

5. *Omit Filling Out Forms*

Since most counseling agencies begin by having the counselee fill out information forms, you may feel you should do so too if you are to be somewhat "professional." You may be glad, it is true, for some of the information a problem checklist or a personal prejudice checklist discloses. But as a lay counselor, from your stance as a concerned fellow Christian, printed forms may be more of a hindrance than an asset at the outset. You probably already know a great deal of what the form would disclose. As new pertinent information emerges you can jot it down in your own chosen format. Many of the validated forms require you to hold membership in a certain accrediting association if you are to use them, and many forms are so complicated that the counselee finds them forbidding. Tests have merit in group work and in agencies in which many persons need to get to know a given counselee. But they are always quite secondary to the deep personal interview.

If you do keep files and records of your work with your counselees, use only initials and never full names. Keep any confidential material under lock and key and destroy it when counseling is terminated.

Occasionally you will have a counselee who does not mind if you tape record the interview. If you later write down a summary of your best recall of the interview, and only then go back and listen to the actual recording of it, you can discover how selective your own memory is. You can force yourself to ask, Why did I forget this aspect or that? Why did I respond so poorly? It is only by such severe and unrelenting self-discipline that you move toward the self-awareness and skill which will make you a professional in the best sense of the word.

6. *Set Your Time Limits in Advance*

You will be wise to limit interviews to one hour. Running on and on wastes time and surfaces more material than can be processed.

It is important that both you and your counselee agree on the amount of time available for an interview. If you have another appointment which you must meet in forty minutes, and you wait until the thirty-fifth minute to disclose this, your counselee may feel hurried, rejected, and put off by you. If you weaken and allow the session to drag on for fear you will offend the counselee, then you will be preoccupied, frustrated, and a poor counselor. Most counselees are poor gaugers of time during a counseling session. You are wise to sit where you can see a clock without too obviously keeping check on the time. You will help both your counselees and yourself to terminate the interview with a sense of wrap-up and security if you say something like, "I see we have five minutes yet to go."

Quite often counselees will hold back their crucial questions for most of the hour and then "dump them on you" just when the hour is up. Keep a record of such questions and promise to return to them later. Remind your counselees that the opportunity to grow continues between sessions, and that you will be giving serious thought to the unresolved issues. You are seldom wise to allow the counseling session to drag on beyond the agreed upon hour.

7. *Clarify Your Contract or Covenant*

It is your responsibility as counselor to clarify your mutual understandings about precisely "what is going on here." Each of you obviously has expectations. Counseling can begin, proceed, and terminate with the most courtesy and best results if your mutual assumptions are clarified. State your understanding of the covenant between yourself and the counselee in the simplest, least pompous, and least threatening terms possible. Be clear in your own mind what you have to offer, what the counselee has already tried, and what contract could and should be entered into to provide real help. When you clarify and structure the session, you are demonstrating to your counselees the value of discipline, organization, and carefulness in coping with problems.

✳ Following are some illustrations of simple contracts. "It is my understanding that I am agreeing to walk with you through this problem you are raising. I understand that we will use a simple interview approach and see whether you find your solution in one or two sessions. If you and I feel longer time is needed then we can plan for a longer series. [It might be well here to suggest the number of sessions you propose.] You can expect from me that I will keep absolutely confidential anything you say, I will never take the responsibility away from you, I will help you to find your strengths and resources to solve your problem, and I will suggest another counselor if matters come up in which I feel I cannot be of help." Be very explicit and clear about the time to be spent in a given session.

A simpler covenant or contract might be, "Let's devote an hour each week for the next [agreed upon number of] weeks to seek a solution to your problem. You will be open, honest, and continue to take the responsibility for your problem. I will keep it confidential, give it everything I've got, and be honest with you if I feel you should seek help elsewhere." Be sure to have your counselees participate in your setting of the goals and contract for your hours together. You can take a complaint and transform it into a goal or objective.

Some cultural analysts suggest that middle-class

people tend to trust a person if he has lots of diplomas, degrees, credentials, and proof of professional training. To meet this expectancy, some counselors literally line the wall behind their desk with their many diplomas. On the other hand, persons from the poor class, who often have experienced oppression by the rich and the strong, tend to trust because of relationships of honesty and warm caring.

A part of your contract is a simple agreement to meet for about so long, for a stated purpose, with specific expectations, and agreed-upon limitations to achieve certain goals. The contract is a means to a larger end and then the contract passes out of existence. But if you and your counselee are in Christ together, and your interaction is actually a sharing in His divine life and love, then your relationship is part of a larger covenant. A covenant is an end itself, and not merely a means to an end.

Sometimes it is useful for you as counselor to ask the counselee how he or she is perceiving the agreement between you.

8. *Sense When One Interview Is Sufficient*

You should not attempt to "seduce" every potential counselee into a long counseling relationship just because you enjoy counseling and because you know that human problems tend to connect with the depth of the other individual. Some persons receive all of the help they need through one well-guided interview. Reserve your counseling time for those persons who really do need a sustained relationship, carried through repeated interviews, to solve a serious problem.

How can you tell when one interview will do? By the close of one interview you should have noted some of the following factors. Do both the counselee and you have a clear grasp of what the problem is, or is it still confused? Is the counselee stable and strong enough emotionally to solve the problem? Does the counselee seem to have the necessary facts in hand to make an intelligent decision? Does the counselee seem reasonably free from emotional blocking? Is the rapport between you good?

If the answers to questions such as the above are "yes," your task as counselor is to assist in a commonsense solving of a problem. Your task is to walk alongside of the counselee during each necessary stage of a complete act or thought. But do not let your first impressions become firm too soon. Keep you mind open until all of the necessary evidence is in. Keep pace with your counselee.

First help identify the problem. Then analyze its possible causes. Next look at its implications. Notice who is involved, for how long, with how much emotion. Observe whether a decision is premature, ripe now, or already long-delayed. Be sure you are doing a two-sided evaluation, facing the facts on both sides of the issue, as tough-mindedly as an expert debating team would do it.

Then help the counselee brainstorm the possible solution, listing all he or she has been thinking about. You as counselor might add to the list, "Have you thought of trying—?" Each hypothesis or proposed solution should be put forth as clearly, as concisely, and as honestly as possible. Keep asking yourself and your counselee, Are these all of the constructive, viable solutions to the problem?

The next stage is to help the counselee pretest, and count the cost of each solution. Insist that the counselee complete such sentences as, "If I decide to do that, it will mean that—'' Help the counselee consider realistically what a given solution will cost to himself or herself, to other people important in his life, and to his relationship with God. There is something about really knowing the full truth about a choice which has to be made which sets the choosing person free.

The next step is for the counselee to choose. Usually this should be done decisively, taking notice of mingled feeling which remains. But beware if your counselee is merely on a "head trip" and is trying to solve a real problem with little emotional involvement.

The final stage is to plan an appropriate series of steps to carry out the decision.

The five-step sequence listed above is the bony framework of the problem solving interview. Your job as counselor is to help the counselee not to bypass any of the steps. Meanwhile keep alert for missing gaps of information, any distortions, blind spots, rationalizations, evasions, and any dishonesty toward self or others involved.

If your counselee's problem solving seems distorted in some way, or if the person's decision-making powers seem deadlocked in some inner filibuster, then it is proper to observe that more time, a slower pace, and more sessions may be needed. Suggest that you renegotiate your contract or covenant for a longer range counseling relationship. Deeper counseling needs to move through a phase when relationship is built, then a phase when problems are weighed, before solutions can be tested.

Certain problem areas almost always call for a series of interviews. Vocational choice should not be decided in one interview, but needs to be an intermittent process.

Grief counseling lengthens out simply because the grief process can't be hurried. A marriage problem which has a long history is almost never solved in one session.

When you are convinced that the problem is long-standing and serious, and the counselee is so intent upon solving it that a series of interviews is called for, you may be wise to suggest a series of six interviews, one each week, for an hour each session. Even though the problem will not be "solved" then, a deliberate pause to evaluate progress is always useful after six interviews. Many counseling agencies are finding that the series of six interviews is the most suitable for the majority of their counselees.

9. *Prepare a Religious History of Your Counselee*

When you and the counselee have agreed that the problem is too elusive or far-reaching to be worked through in one interview, and you set a covenant-contract for four or six counseling sessions, you may be wise to devote one session to taking a religious history. Only a quack in the medical field will give medicine without first making a careful diagnosis. Only a quack in the counseling field will accept a solution to a counselee's problem without understanding its causes and its roots.

Explain to your counselees that you want to take a religious history to enable you to understand them and their problem in the greatest possible depth. Lengthen or shorten the history depending on the importance of the material you uncover.

Begin the religious history by asking your counselees to describe their childhood notions of God, some early good and bad memories of religion, who it was who gave them their religious ideas, and how they feel now about those same persons. Observe whether their early religion was legalistic, punitive, moralistic, magical, or in other ways hurtful.

Ask your counselees to trace the high points of their religious pilgrimage during junior and adolescent years. Paraphrase and reflect back what you hear them saying about their awakenings, guilts, relapses, conversion experiences, and how religion functioned in relation to their sexuality, their desires for status, their search for vocation, love, excitement, power, and meaning.

Some counselors expect to find the mother's taboos interiorized in areas of sex, dirt, polite speech, and nudity. They look for evidence of the father's taboos in areas of breaking things, talking back, stealing, fighting, and respecting authority figures. Draw out the taboos your counselee actually has brought from childhood, but be careful not to impose any theory upon what you find.

As you review your counselee's religious history observe what crises affected faith, how vocational choice either did or did not become a faith issue, how their faith impinged upon their courtship and marriage, and how their devotional habits changed after they shared a bedroom with a marriage partner. Watch for prejudices, guilts, insecurities, evasion devices, as well as strengths, hidden talents, and genuine growth areas in the lives of your counselees.

A religious history should take careful notice of any changes of church affiliation and the meaning this held. Times of renewal or recommitment should be probed. Struggles with doubt can reveal a great deal about the counselee. The impact of higher education upon the childish faith of early years, the way faith coped with the death of loved ones, with religious extremism, and with times of personal failure—all these can come out as counselees trace their religious pilgrimage. Analysts and therapists still devoted to Freudian views place most weight upon early childhood experiences. But the experiences of youth and early adult years are now given priority by many counselors.

A religious history should probe the counselee's feelings about the church, its requirements, its fellowship, its preaching, its goodness, its hypocracy, its ability to help, and other such interests. This will help you as counselor to evaluate the place of the church as a spiritual resource in your counselee's life.

While listening to the counselee's religious history, you can be observing many other crucial factors in addition to those recited. By reading between the lines and listening to tonal and body language, you can learn a great deal about self-blame, perfectionism, scrupulosity, or defiance and rebellion. You can detect if there are feelings of worthlessness, self-despising, or self-punishing. Purposeful forgetting and selective remembering are common, and what your counselee still remembers out of childhood can be very revealing.

Notice also tendencies toward exaggeration or indecision, reliance upon magic, or irrational fears. You may detect problems of suspiciousness, resentment, manic tendencies, deviousness, escapisms, rigidity, or the need to show off.

As counselor you know that "God's grace can triumph" and that "all princes do limp." It will be useful for you to know just how your counselee does limp, so you can help God's grace to overcome the problems in his unique life.

Help your counselees utilize strengths from their own

religious history in solving their present problem. Notice how they overcame inferiority feelings. How did they help to modify their own parents? How did they claim their own place, their spot of turf, and their place in the sun? What "road map" offered to them in childhood are they still following or denying? What have they modified in the "right-wrong" code they inherited? What is their way of changing their functioning conscience?

How did your counselee do in life's "trial-run" in male-female relationships—the family? How were the lessons of competition learned, or not learned in sibling rivalries? How did he learn to treat a woman, or she learn to treat a man?

While you are listening, deeply and intently, and asking crucial questions about what you are hearing, think of yourself as a "good detective." Don't look for evidence to convict, but for evidence of growth, slumbering potential, assets of which they are unaware, and for ways God's grace has worked in their lives in their own past. Look for their coping patterns, their way of solving problems, and for residual strengths.

If your counselee resents doing a religious history, don't insist or force the issue. Simply begin with the present problem and when it seems essential, delve back into the history of that particular concern. If at one stage of counseling you trace back a counselee's experiences with authority figures, and at another time his or her experience with overcoming fears or guilts, you can soon piece together a picture of the person's spiritual pilgrimage.

Be sure you have identified the central problem you want to work on, whether you utilize a religious history to establish its background or not.

10. *Consciously Rely on the Leading of the Holy Spirit*

This is an attitude of supreme importance for your counseling. Almost every activity of the Holy Spirit seems "tailor-made" to strengthen your counseling relationships. Many Christians know intellectually what the Holy Spirit does within the believer and between Christians. But when the Spirit's activity is deliberately invoked, almost moment by moment, during your counseling, amazing enrichments and possibilities are opened.

When you attempt to counsel another person, think of yourself as an assistant to God's Holy Spirit in the realm of the human spirit, much as a medical doctor who is thoroughly Christian regards himself as an assistant to the restorative powers God placed in the human body. God's Spirit is already at work in the depth of the human spirit—calling, converting, wooing, seeking to heal and to bless. Align yourself with the Holy Spirit and ask to become an agent in this process. In such an effort you are truly a laborer together with God. Continue rigorous self-examination during your counseling to be sure your own inner life is honest and growing toward Christlikeness.

Rely upon God's Spirit to lay bare the thoughts and intents of the hearts of both yourself and the counselee. As you counsel, breathe a silent prayer that the Spirit will decode the deepest groanings which cannot be uttered so that even unverbalized needs may be sensed. The Spirit will teach you what to say when you are at your wit's end before the mystery and profundity of the human spirit. The Spirit can help you to hear in "the language in which the counselee was born" so that present words converge with meanings buried deep in the memories of childhood.

As a Christian counselor you long for the ability to

bring the truth as it exists in the words and deeds of Jesus to bear upon the baffling problems and ethical ambiguities of the life of the counselee. The Spirit can bring to remembrance meanings from what Jesus taught, at a level far deeper than the mere correct quoting of memorized verses. It is the Spirit's work to convict of sin, of righteousness (God's right way to go), and of the end result of a path of action (judgment to come). Only the all-wise Spirit of an omniscient God can know what is right for each unique person in each unique circumstance. If you can trust God's Spirit to speak His will to the heart of the counselee, then you can resist more easily the peril of becoming the answer man, of playing God, of telling the counselee what to do, or even of plastering a Scripture verse upon an undiagnosed infection of the human spirit.

When God's Spirit is calling your counselees to move forward in a risky new step of faith, they can dare to believe that somehow all things will work together for good. They can dare to "go out not knowing."

The working of the Holy Spirit should be invoked anew during a stalemate. Often the breakthrough in the deadlocked problem-solving process in the heart of the counselee comes as the decision is made to really "call Jesus Lord" in a new area. At some new call to obedience persons are able to take up their cross. The Spirit enables them to "call Jesus Lord" in the hard decisions of life involving money, power, affluence, sex, pride, vocation, family, business, or amusement.

As a Christian counselor you do not only believe that the Holy Spirit once loosened inhibitions on the day of Pentecost. You also expect the Spirit to relax specific inhibitions of bashfulness brought along from childhood, or of sexual inhibitions which are frustrating an otherwise pure marriage, or of the inability to express feelings which is drying up conversations in the family. Consciously seek for this slight relaxing of inhibitions as you counsel up-tight people.

When the counselee has poured out more than he can process, and feels crushed by the weight of life's problems, or feels abandoned by family and friends and is hurting badly, then both you and the counselee can specifically invoke the working of God's Spirit as Comforter.

The Holy Spirit can "drive to utterance," inspiring you to speak when a "teachable moment" has come. The Spirit can annoint and empower a gentle word of probing, a pointed question, an option to be considered, a confrontation to expose a falsehood, or a summary of what is "seeming good to the Holy Ghost and to us."

Both you and your counselees, if all are consciously Christian, will be relying upon the Holy Spirit to heighten knowledge and insight, overcome shyness and inhibition, give freedom and flexibility, increase concentration, guide timing, heal embarrassment, bring conviction, actualize forgiveness, and empower for decision and action. These ministries of God's Holy Spirit can become the very essence of effective, life-transforming counseling.

11. *Refer Persons Who Are Seriously Psychotic*

As counselor remain alert for signs of high anxiety, unusual distrust, an unexplained sense of guilt or shame, or inappropriate feelings of inferiority. If the sense of identity is strong and clear, begin from there and start to look for causes of these persistent emotions. If persons have no clear sense of identity, begin to draw out their personal histories to give them a sense of who they are. Explore how they use their sense of gifts, of call, of vocation, and of goals to help them focus their identity.

If you begin to suspect that a counselee needs sustained therapy, if you observe bizarre actions, undue withdrawal and soliloquy, hearing of voices, extreme and irrational fears, constant wide swings of emotion from highs to suicidal depression, a lost contact with reality, inability to make decisions, a sense of isolation, or threats to self and others, do not hesitate to refer him or her to a professional therapist.

3

SKILLS IN RESPONDING AND INTERVENING IN COUNSELING

1. *Listen Intently*

Try to give to your counselee the full power of sustained and loving attention. This is one of the greatest gifts one person can give to another. Focus all the powers of your mind and emotions like a spotlight upon what your counselee intends to say. Deliberately jerk your mind back from its inevitable "wool gathering" and wandering. Be acutely aware that your mind thinks three times faster than your counselee can talk. If you cannot get victory over wandering attention any other way, try asking your counselee's forgiveness each time your mind has wandered.

Be praying for divine healing from the hardening of your mind's categories. Admit that your mind inevitably has its own prejudices, and these can prejudge what your counselee is trying to say. Keep on listening even when you are astonished and puzzled, and when your thoughts can find no answer for what you are hearing. Be ready for mystery and for wonder as you listen. God's Spirit blows where it will when giving new births of insight within your counselee. Don't expect to understand all that is going on between God's Spirit and your counselee in the unplumbed depths. Keep your eye contact steady, tender, and not too piercing, so the counselee is comfortable under your gaze.

Listen carefully for what your counselee is trying to say, is intending to say, and wishes could be said. Try to hear the "inner dialogue" of the counselee. Listen to your counselee the way you hope God listens to your prayers. Let this be your model for active listening, and never, never stop disciplining yourself toward deeper and still deeper hearing. Keep reminding yourself that the story your counselee is telling you is likely only part of the total story. Keep listening for the total story.

Be aware that all counselors hear less fairly when they are overly tired. You may miss hearing (due to fatigue) what the person is hoping to become. You may not hear what his "I" is trying to say to your own "Thou." You may miss the question behind his question. Tremendous energy in full focus is required to listen "with your third ear," to be receiving "vibes" from another total person to your total person. Keep praying for this quiet miracle to be happening. If you feel too exhausted to keep giving the intense attention which all good counseling requires, you should admit it and get some rest.

Be alert as you listen, not only to the words your counselee expresses, but to the deeper groanings which cannot be uttered. Consider how much of your counselee's responses are on an intellectual level, and how much on an emotional level. What are the little half-formed "sentences in the head" saying?

Still deeper than your counsclees' sex drives or power hungers may be their place or "territorial imperative." Your counselees may be searching for their own "spot of turf," their own "place to stand," their own "demilitarized zone" where they are safe to be themselves, their own bit of "free space" which is absolutely their own. If you feel your counselees have found their own "place to be" and their "freedom to be me," then notice carefully whether they know how to exist before God. Can they admit that they exist as from God their Creator? Can they stand before God in solitary and life transforming meeting? Can they accept partnership with God so they move out for God? Or have they individuated only to become lonely existentialists? Is their's a solitary flight of the "alone into the alone?" Do they feel that they are "on vacation from eternity" because they are intensely aware that they "come from God and go to God?"

In your deep listening notice whether one part of their life has risen up and asserted dominance over the whole. Does their desire to compete blot out their desire to cooperate? Does their interest in sex obscure their interest in prayer? Does their desire for fellowship and community obscure their desire for solitude? Carl Jung called this a "complex." You need not label it in order to be alert to it. Just what is your counselee appealing for? What is the help he or she wants?

As a counselor you will need to keep listening to your counselees' sense of their own limits. What sets limits to their free space? What walls are they colliding with which seem to decree, Thus far and no farther? Are they accepting limits too passively? Are they defying limits like a Lucifer saying, "I will be as God"? Are your counselees coping with stress by bravado, avoidance, suspiciousness, regression, or depression? Are your counselees working at their problems in an organized way, or striking out blindly? Are they realistic about the limits within which they must live out their lives? Your counselees' daydreams and fantasies may reveal as much about them as their night dreams.

2. *Offer Acceptance and Understanding*

When you sit facing your counselee, your whole manner and being should say, "I understand how you are feeling right now. You may think you are all alone on the little solitary spot of turf where you are standing, but actually I am right there with you. I understand what you are feeling. You are not alone in what you are going through right now." That assurance that "I do know how you feel" is the essence of understanding in counseling.

Try to reassure your counselee that "if I were going through what you are going through, I would likely feel just as you are feeling. Right now I don't want to change you. Tell me what changes you want to make, and I'll try to help you make them." Often when such nonjudgmental acceptance is experienced and deeply felt, the counselee will panic for a little while. All his defenses are now useless. He is accepted "just as I am without one plea." He must decide if he wishes, deep down, to change. He must decide if he wishes to change for his own sake, and not merely to yield to pressures.

You may be saying, "But what if I can't really understand and accept like that?" You can always go back to God's fountain of nonjudgmental love, receive again God's forgiveness for your failure, and hopefully be renewed in the power to give accepting love. It is truly a demanding task to keep constantly valuing your counselees, being concerned about your counselees, caring for your counselees, prizing, respecting, and liking them even when they cannot yet be giving the same to you in return. Some counselors insist that they must receive fees and be constantly aware that the counselee is paying them well if they, as counselors, are to go on giving such costly acceptance. I personally do not feel that such a "hireling" attitude helps at all. Such love cannot finally be bought or paid for. By its very nature it must be free.

If you read widely in the literature on counseling, you will discover that some counselors try to give an acceptance which is essentially neutral. They offer acceptance which is midway between praise and blame; somewhere between a yes and a no; or a balancing act between giving approval and giving disapproval. But if you and your counselee are both members of Christ's body, committed together to Christ's will and way for a style of life, any pretense of neutrality will be hard for you to maintain. You can, however, hold yourself back from telling your counselee what he must do. Only his Lord can finally do that. It may be that Christ will reveal His will through the consensus of your counselee and yourself.

Keep sensitive to undue dependency. If a counselee begins to phone you between sessions, write to you, and ask to see you often and for long sessions, you may be snared into a dependency pattern. Examine your own heart. Do you subtly want to play God? Are you flattered by having this counselee consider you so wise and helpful? Deal honestly with any tendency you discover within yourself to want to be the great "guru" upon whom folks depend! If you can't work through this, you may need to go for counseling yourself. If you subtly think of yourself as "the great helper with the x-ray eyes," you are in real need of help yourself.

It is crucial that your unconditional acceptance continues no matter what your counselees reveal to you. Some counselors can easily give acceptance while their counselees pour out problems related to health, or learning, or grieving. But just let a counselee admit to forgery, or homosexuality, or feelings of demon possession, and the counselor's inner spirit recoils in shock and withdraws to "safety." All this is keenly sensed by the counselee and understood as rejection.

3. *Expect Open Sharing and Catharsis*

In your counseling relationship try not to let your counselee "pour it all out" too soon. Such "show and tell" may be premature. The person may indeed pour out more than can be processed adequately and comfortably worked through. The counselee may go away feeling guilty, betrayed, denuded, angry, and taken advantage of. Confession and dealing with real sin during counseling sessions is often necessary and very important, but it requires great tact on your part. It is important that you as counselor also know how to move through a "confession stage" in your own thrusts of growth, if you are to deal wisely with your counselees in theirs.

You should be ready to call a halt when the counselee has poured out all that you can reasonably deal with that day. Help the counselee achieve some cleansing of guilty and painful memories which have surfaced before you invite more confession. Watch for any false exhibitionism when a counselee is confessing. Is the counselee trying to shock you? Move carefully, prayerfully, and reverently here. Does your counselee seem to be getting some satisfaction as he pours out his soul? Does what he is saying have a certain rehearsed quality? Is he bragging about himself?

Ask yourself whether your counselee has had a habit of telling it like it is, and of frank openness. Sense whether the counselee is ready to begin working seriously to correct the things he or she is confessing. Is your counselee one who has been "going forward" in every revival meeting, and claiming the "hot seat" in every sensitivity lab? You will need to insist upon sincerity and honesty, coupled with a realistic desire to change. Mere ventilation and confession may do little real good. Continually examine your own heart to be sure that you do not take a morbid delight in listening to gory or sordid confessions. You, as counselor, can help to turn your counselee's confession toward solving the central problem. You may need to help sort out the central problem from a cluster of peripheral ones.

When listening to your counselee's confessions, watch for any "little atonement rituals" being used. Has your counselee been assigning little acts of penance to himself or herself, little self-punishments, or doing little "deeds of merit" to earn forgiveness?

Do not merely give sympathy, or allow your counselee to cry on your shoulder. Empathy is much more helpful than mere sympathy, but includes all that is of value in sympathy. The counselee is not really helping himself move forward if he indulges in repeated self-denunciation. Do not too readily believe all your counselee says when pouring out his inner feelings under intense emotion. It is easy to exaggerate at such times. Listen, love, and wait, and avoid coming to premature conclusions.

What about making restitution? Again and again your counselees will ask how much "making things right" they should do. Some will want to go all out and restore fourfold everyone they ever wronged. Others will want not only a very secret confession, but secret restitution, keeping it secret from the actual person they have wronged! You will have only a few basic principles and your Spirit-directed intuition to guide you on specific cases. There is no book of penance to which you can turn. Few things reveal more about your counselees' inner life than their number of guilty secrets, and what they are doing about them. Beware of attempting to work on too many issues at the same time. This only causes confusion.

One principle to guide both you and your counselee is that it is wholesome to be forthright and courageous in making restitutions, as far as possible, to specific persons they have wronged. But at the same time the counselor should not demand that the counselee must make restituion. Restitution is an area where one needs to be stern with oneself and lenient with others.

A second principle is that your counselee's restitution should not be a "work of merit so as to buy salvation." Forgiveness is given freely through Christ and His people. Neither Christ nor you dare be heard to say, "I

80

will forgive you if you make just the right amount of restitution." Try to communicate unconditional forgiveness as you encourage your counselee to make appropriate restitution for past sins.

Ask your counselees for whose sake they might want to make restitution. If it is to restore the good name of the church, this could be a wholesome motivation. If it is to reduce hurting on the part of the person wronged, this can be useful. If it is to remove coolness in relationship with the persons wronged, this might be a good reason to do it. It is, of course, your counselees' decision. Your task as counselor is to help them to think it through, and to keep out of their way while they make a free decision on their own.

Some counselors call it "religious guilt" when a counselee cannot feel forgiven by God, and "psychological guilt" when the counselee cannot forgive himself. As counselor you are equally concerned to help your counselees achieve both, but you begin with the vertical relationship problem because it is basic to the second, interior one.

4. *Be Supportive and Offer Forgiveness in Advance*

Take care to be especially supportive during the phase of your counseling sessions when confession and repentance are going on. Counselees need to know that you are carrying them in intercessory prayer as they go on admitting their needs. By nodding your head you can be implying, "I'm hearing you. Go on. It's safe, I'm with you."

You can be supportive with remarks like, "I know it takes courage for you to talk like this" or "I admire your honesty." Offering yourself to be available can be a support, such as, "If you want to work further at that matter, I'll be glad to assist you in thinking it through."

Try to increase your tact and skill in helping counselees to "cleanse their memories." As you help your counselee relive a painful memory, all the while lift it up to Jesus Christ in confessional, meditative prayer. You may also get into this while taking a religious history. Some crises may cause your counselee to regress to an earlier and painful attitude of scrupulosity, shame, or self-despising.

Try to stand by and assist tactfully if your counselee begins wrestling with feelings of persistent guilt. Keep in mind all you already know about what has formed (or even deformed) your counselee's conscience. It may be that early teachings of legalistic taboos have produced a guilt-ridden conscience. If you are convinced that this is the case, you may attempt reverently to reeducate your counselee's conscience in line with true freedom in Christ.

Go very slowly in encouraging your counselee to move contrary to his or her own conscience. Only God by His Holy Spirit should reset a Christian's conscience. It would be better, if your counselee's conscience needs reeducating, that it be done at another time than during an emotionally laden counseling session.

If it becomes clear that your counselee is struggling with real guilt because of real sin against God and neighbor, then you can help your counselee to own the guilt before yourself and before God, repudiate the sin in a clear word of confession, and—if that is called for— plan an appropriate act of restitution. Then you can speak the word of absolution which helps forgiveness to feel real.

5. *Use Enabling and Drawing Out Responses*

In assisting your counselees in their search for insight and solution, you can offer a broad opening, such as, "Is there something more you'd like to talk about?" or "What more do you feel we should discuss?" Be careful not to run ahead of your counselee.

You can assist your counselee by asking for needed data or description. This can help your counselee to think it through. "What happened then?" "How did you feel ✓ then?" "Can you help me to understand just how it was?"

Sometimes you can help your counselee by encouraging a comparison. "Were your feelings something like—?" "What were your experiences like?" "Who does the person who is troubling you remind you of?" Be fully human, and keep listening for the deeply human responses. But beware lest your use of comparisons lead your counselee on a long and fruitless detour.

You can enable your counselees in their search for insight by linking together common elements. Call to their attention common themes and elements you are hearing in their story. Point out apparent cause and effect sequences. "As I've been listening to you, I've been noticing that all of your clashes have been about money" (or about men, promptness, or whatever). Try to link some of your counselee's distressing complaints with a more basic, casual problem.

You can sometimes help when your counselee reaches a plateau or an impasse and does not seem able to go on. You can suggest and honor a time of silence for introspection and reflection. You can suggest praying about the matter until the next session. You can suggest collaboration. ("It might help if you could bring me in on that matter which is making you pause.") If your counselee is hesitating to be sure that two-sided and fair consideration is happening, you can strongly affirm this effort. Your counselee should not only be discovering new angles of his or her problem, but also new resources for a new beginning.

You, as counselor, can focus on one matter which seems to you to be crucial, but which is in danger of getting lost. "I believe that particular matter is important," or "I feel that this point deserves more attention." Often, as counselor, you will focus upon a wrong attitude of the counselee, believing that after his or her outlook is improved, the surface problem can be readily solved.

Sometimes you will help the counselee forward if you translate a bare fact into the feelings which go with it. "And so you feel very lonely," or "And so you are wondering why this is the case in your life?"

But use probing responses sparingly. You are not a prosecuting attorney cross-examining a witness. Probing responses can frighten a counselee during the early sessions of a counseling relationship. Probing can be painful during the deepest exploratory sessions. You need to be very tactful and tender in your probing responses like, "I wonder why you did that," or "I wonder what your motive was in saying that," or "I wonder what you were thinking when that happened?" (Questions which ask why, what, where, when or how are probes.)

Since your goal is to keep attention focused on the counselee you can often do that by silent attention, waiting for your counselee to proceed, or by a murmured response, "Mm-mm-mm."

Many counselees will regress and retreat from a solution because it feels more comfortable to remain in their quandry than to risk a costly adventure or solution. If you sense manipulative or retreating behavior, you can point this out to them.

When you discover that counselees are treating you in some of the same nonproductive ways which are helping to cause the problem, this can be called to their attention. Expect and accept much of this transference during the early stages of counseling.

If your counselees seem about to despair because their problems seem so rare and so hopeless, you can remind them that they are not unique, their kind of problem has been met and conquered before, and that you are not despairing.

Sometimes a counselee may play it safe by inviting you to give an opinion about a problem a friend has, or something "then and there" rather than a "here and now" problem of his own. Firmly, but kindly, refuse to discuss the problem of someone else.

6. *Respond Tenderly and Carefully*

When you hold the mirror, as it were, and reflect back how your counselees come through to you, you are more than a mere echo. Even though you add nothing new, you tend to reveal to your counselees how they really are coming across. Your reflection and restatement of what your counselees have said reveal meanings between the lines, attitudes that shine through. Your counselees may feel as if they were under an x-ray of their very soul. If you restate with deep sensitivity and tact, your counselees often gain insight into themselves. Reflecting back to your counselee just how you are hearing and experiencing them is a powerful, strong response, to be done only in an attitude of prayerful love.

When you probe still deeper by interpreting what you think your counselees mean, then you come very close to seizing the initiative of the interview away from your counselees. Your counselees may lapse into silence and wait for you to lecture and to give the answers. Be careful when you interpret what you think your counselees feel, think, and mean to say that you are not dominating your counselees. If you come on too strongly, and your counselees are weak or confused, they may passively allow you to do their thinking for them. Be reverent as you interpret. Do only a little of it at a time. Be sure your counselees are with you before you move on. Merely suggest your interpretation; never decree it. Do not play God.

Offering explanations to your counselees of why they did certain things, of what their behavior actually reveals, or of the limits of their freedom in their present situation—all these are risky. Your counselees may feel that you are trying to give a verdict. Suggesting the humorous or ridiculous aspects of your counselees' behavior is usually unwise. Humor is likely to hurt unless it is used with great sensitivity and tact.

Offering encouragement to your counselees seems such a good and altogether innocent thing to do that you are tempted to be lavish in it. Why not spur them on, back them up, and tell them they are doing a good job of problem solving? But when you offer encouragement too freely, you also offer subtle pressure to conform. You seem to be taking responsibility and trying to lead. This can make your counselees dependent upon you, and suggest that they need your help to keep them going. Strong encouragement comes mighty close to urging, and are the counselees who succumb to urging really free?

When using any of the "strong responses" described above, read your counselee's reactions to them moment by moment, constantly breathing a prayer and relying upon the help of God's Spirit so that you truly understand what is going on deep within your counselee. Often there will be resistances, sometimes anger, sometimes new insights. Truly the "wind blows where it will" when new life and strength are coming to birth within a person.

As counselor, sit humbly and reverently before this mystery. Inspirational pep talks are of almost no value in counseling. They do belong within catechism, teaching, preaching, and fellowship.

Giving actual suggestions and advice are so risky in counseling that you must examine very carefully why you would do so and when. Your counselees may already have collected more advice than they know what to do with. Why do they need yours to add to their collection? Will you secretly resent it if they don't follow your advice? If they take your advice and act upon it, will they have an autonomous decision, an act of their own will based upon their own insight and decision? Will any decision they make upon your advice be a lasting decision? Do you like to have people advising you what you ought to do? Your counselees may interpret your advice-giving as urging, or even cajoling. If you attach morals or Bible verses to your advice, you bring strong pressure upon them. Do you like to make your decisions that way? Advice-giving can be part of your mutual friendship sharing occasions, when you both give and receive advice freely. But advice-giving has almost no place within the deep relationship of structured counseling.

Still stronger and more confrontational responses are used by some counselors. They criticize their counselees, tell them when they disbelieve them, ridicule them, and even threaten rejection if their counselees dare to differ or to reach opposing conclusions. These attitudes are so dangerous and so foreign to the inner spirit of true counseling that they should not be included among counseling responses at all. Most of these responses elevate the counselor as the authority and belittle the counselee's dignity. The counselees feel they will be rejected unless they conform. Such counseling is experienced as scolding or a threat. Counselees hear in it a command and a threat of punishment if they do not obey.

Timing responses tactfully is crucial. When you say a given thing may be just as important as what you say. The counselees readiness to hear often makes the difference.

Asking your counselee to role play both parties in his conflict is a "strong response." Only imaginative and courageous counselees can do it. But often help comes as a counselee speaks out the one feeling he has for a while, and then takes another chair and argues back from his other side or his other feeling. These techniques are called "thought stoppers."

If your counselee is considering behavior which may harm someone else, ask him to switch roles and be the target person for a while, talking out how that feels.

7. *Respect Periods of Silence*

A time of silence during a counseling session can have many widely different meanings. The counselee may stand aghast at what has come gushing out, and stay silent in remorse and shame. "As long as my guilty secret was held in my inner shrine of loneliness, no one else but God could know. But now I've let the secret out. It cannot be recalled. What will happen next? Now I am forced to deal with my guilt." If these thoughts are spinning inside your counselee's head during a time of silence, try in a low-key way to help the person verbalize these feelings. Keep on praying; keep on listening; keep on offering acceptance. A gentle comment may help, such as, "I see you are finding it hard to continue. Can you put your thoughts into words?" or "Is there something more you wish to say?" Counselees who seem most eager for help often are most hesitant to enter the deep relationship which the securing of real help requires.

Maybe your counselee really has finished. Every counselee "peels his own onion," decides how many layers of inner life to share, and has a right to privacy. Accept that for the present. Deeply hidden secrets sometimes keep coming out after ten and even twelve sessions, even though each session was vital and dealing with real stuff. Don't reach out and physically touch your counselees to get them started again. The intimacy represented by touching may release a lot of other dynamics all at once.

Sometimes the counselee will lapse into silence because your own attention has drifted away. Some anxiety within yourself has been stirred up. You were feverishly trying to cope with your own unsolved problems in the same problem area. You were no longer really listening and so your counselee stopped talking. If honest introspection reveals that this is indeed true, then manage to quiet your own inner ear again, until you can give the gift of total attention.

If your counselee has just plumbed a new depth of a

painful memory, or an equally painful prospect of the furture, then you will be wise to sit quietly and suffer in silence with your counselee. There are moments when suffering silence is more eloquent than speech. "Say, that must hurt terribly!" or "I hear you and I'm hurting with you," or simply your tears may punctuate the silence. Be as transparent as you can be about the qualities that make persons human. By modeling patience yourself, you can help teach your counselee to be patient.

Rarely should you as counselor break a silence when you can't sense what the silence really means. Don't rush in, like Peter, and talk when you don't know what to say. Don't glibly reassure that, "I know just how you feel." If, however, you have sensed what the silence means, and you can put that meaning into words, this is truly helpful.

8. *Use Direct Questions Sparingly*

Too many counselors rely upon direct questioning. Many persons come for counseling expecting you to ask questions to get the facts, and then to give advice to provide the answers. Tactful counseling uses direct questions sparingly, and tries to avoid giving advice indirectly by loading a series of questions a certain way.

Your direct questions tend to lead the inquiry where you as counselor want to go, but this may not be where the counselee's hurting is coming from. You unconsciously imply the answer you want. But in so doing you foreclose or shut off other leads. Keep monitoring your own feelings and motives while you question your counselee. Just why are you pushing and probing?

Questions requiring "yes" and "no" answers quickly

begin to produce a cross-examination feeling. Your counselees may feel "called on the carpet." Their own search for insight may be hindered. They should learn to be their own detective.

Instead use broad, opening questions to invite your counselees to go on. "Do you have more that you feel like saying?" "Would you care to explore that further?" "Can you say some more about that?" Open-ended questions encourage counselees to pursue insights and feelings still deeper. Beware of compound questions, or a series of questions.

By a gentle, nonthreatening question you can show that you regard something your counselee has said as important worthy of further exploration. "I am sorry I didn't grasp all you were meaning there. Can you spell that out a little more?" A counselee often deepens his or her own grasp of a new insight by repeating it a second time.

If your relationship with your counselees is trusting and comfortable, you can question their understanding of a comment you have made. "Can you tell me in your own words how you understand what I just said?"

Some counselors find it helpful to sketch a parallel (but hypothetical) situation, and invite the counselee to react to it. If your counselee is a person who is good at introspection, try asking him or her what side benefits are coming as a result of the problem! Often there are secondary gains the counselee enjoys.

9. *Avoid Giving Easy Answers*

Even though you give and receive advice freely with fellow members of the congregation as part of your life together, avoid trying to mix advice giving and counseling. Do your advice giving at some other time. In counseling your proper role is to utilize "listening love" and "drawing-out responses" to help the person gain new insights. Your goal is that the counselee can then advise himself or herself from the new insights gained.

Advice usually offers straight, rational, logical, commonsense solutions. But counseling is a process which also evokes and uses the emotional, the nonrational, the intuitive, and the irrational. It traces human feelings to their hang-ups and blockages. Usually unconscious resistances have hindered your counselee from obeying all the good advice of the past.

Do try to perfect your skill and tact in giving advice, in admonishing and in offering guidance. Do offer advice when it is appropriate, when your friend can profit by it, but outside of the counseling-covenanted relationship. When you are counseling, stay by your counseling. As soon as you quit counseling and start giving advice you shut off the flow of your counselee's search for insight. Why go on? It is all settled! The answer is given! Your counselee may pressure you for advice and then unconsciously obey your advice in such a way that it fails to solve the problem! This will "prove" your advice was wrong!

If your counselee demands advice, simply admit that you don't know enough yet to be giving advice to his unique problem, and that advice giving would be inappropriate in the middle of the quest and mutual search in which the two of you are now engaged.

10. *Secure Permission Before Taking Notes or Taping the Conversation*

In some cultures counselees are honored to have a

counselor take notes of what they are saying. Your particular counselee may be cagy about your doing so. If your memory requires notes, frankly say so and ask permission to take a few. You can suggest, "What you are saying is important and I want to remember it accurately. Do you mind if I take a few notes?" and "I can listen to you best if I take a few notes, do you mind?"

Some counselees also take notes and bring their own cassette recorders. What is fair to the one is fair to the other. Just be sure that note-taking is done simply, without distracting from eye contact and personalness.

Don't write down notes about your counselee which you are not willing for the counselee to see. People are sensitive about secret files being kept on them. Your notebook and files about a counselee should be confidential and preferably kept under lock and key.

If your counselee is willing for you to record the interview on tape, make it clear that this is for your benefit alone intended only to assist your memory. Remembering "the little things" the counselee says can become one of your greatest assets as a counselor.

Listening to tapes of your own counseling can be a humbling and instructive experience. Notice how much warmth and concern comes through in your tones. Ask yourself whether you talked too much. Notice any times you interrupted the counselee. Analyze when you started off on another track rather than following up the thing the counselee was obviously interested in. Did you bombard with questions?

Since it is likely that the most of your counselees will feel inhibited if you are recording the interview mechanically, keep training your memory to do its own accurate recording. Get alone briefly, after a counseling session, and recall quickly the crucial moments of the interview. Review in your mind the genuine decisions your counselee reached which you believe might result in change. Make a mental note of any declared intentions which you feel may not be followed through.

11. *Summarize Progress Periodically*

One of the greatest of all skills to learn in the counseling process is the ability to summarize progress. Counseling proceeds imperceptibly, emotions and opinions change quietly below the level of conscious awareness. Few counselees can identify their own progress and claim it unless you as their counselor help them. You should have more objectivity than they so that you can look in fairly upon what has been going on. A summary shows that you are really hearing, both the audible words and the half-denied feelings.

Summarize what you have been feeling as your mutual search has been moving along. Pause periodically and say something like, "It's awfully important to me that I am understanding you fully and deeply. Let me summarize what I have been hearing you say. Correct me if I have heard you only partially or wrongly. I heard you say that so and so happened to you, that you were feeling so and so, and that then you did. . . ." A summary helps to put the parts of the puzzling picture together. Be sure to summarize around the original goals the counselee had in asking for counseling.

Your summary can communicate that you take your counselee's words seriously, that you want to be careful not to distort their meaning, and that your two minds are really moving together at a very deep level. Your summary can ascertain whether your empathy was accurate and whether you actually felt what your counselees were feeling. It can include proposed solutions which you heard implied. Your own words and tones as you summarize will reveal how genuinely you understand and accept your counselee.

In addition to correcting the accuracy of your empathy, your summarizes may chart the ground which has been covered and gained. Often after a clear summary counselees will utter a glad sigh or a word of thanks to God. They see that they are indeed on their way through their problem. They no longer think all is hopeless confusion. Light has broken through. Summaries often help point toward the end of an interview or a series of interviews. Feedback given in a summary is not advice, but another effort to help the counselee come to an autonomous solution.

If you summarize too optimistically, running ahead of where you actually are in your joint problem solving, your counselee may rebuke you, call you back, or lose confidence that you really know the depth of that problem. If, on the contrary, you summarize too darkly and pessimistically, your counselee may become discouraged. Be sure to sense whether your summary feels right and fair to the counselee.

In the later stages of your counseling process you can ask your counselees to summarize the progress and insights gained. Then respond honestly on how this either parallels or differs with what you have been sensing. This method is especially useful with counselees who are insightful, courageous, articulate, and not too intensely emotionalized. If your counselee can prepare a journal entry of a newly gained insight, this helps to fix it in the mind.

Be sure the inner experience and feelings of the counselee are part of any summary. If you sense that you have made mistakes earlier in the counseling process, admit this as part of your summary, so you can calibrate the effect of your errors upon your future sessions.

Be careful in grouping factors during a summary. If you list the pros and cons too vigorously, you sound like a lawyer in court. The very way you group factors in a summary can weight the case unduly.

If you summarize under pros and cons, list the cons first and the pros last so that you close on a hopeful note.

Sometimes in your summary you may point out the sufferings your counselee has undergone and is now undergoing. But alongside of this trace God's providential love and leading in your counselee's life. Summarize also your own feelings as you have walked with your counselee through the hours of deep empathy, caring, and sharing.

If you have heard your counselee imply unrealistic and unattainable goals ("absolutely everybody must like me" or "I must reach perfection") point this out in your summary. An overuse of superlatives like "always" or "never" needs to be reflected back to your counselee.

As a peer counselor in the church you have the right to expect genuine transforming growth and change in personality. If you read much in the fields of therapy and counseling, you will observe the tendency among secular therapists to assume (and even to assert) that only their services bring real changes in personality. Only deep and sustained therapy, they say, re-centers the vital forces within the person. Pastoral counselors should merely be supportive, offer comfort and strength to endure it all, and rally the supporting groups of the church around the counselee. Even more they would doubt that your help as a layman and peer counselor could effect deep change.

But you can be used of God's Spirit to help transform the personality of your counselees if your empathy has been deep and true, your relationship of caring love has been strong and sustained, and you have been honest and tactful and insightful in your summaries. You may not remove any of the basic content of the personality or memory of your counselee. All the hurting memories, the thrusting desires, and crippling inadequacies may still be there. But they will be rearranged into a new form, and so transformed. Where shameful memories have festered, forgiveness can bring release and hope. Where a trauma or suffering of the past has left an inadequacy, new insights may draw strength from that past suffering. The constellation of tensions within your counselee can repolarize around a new center. Life's energies can be refocused around a new faith in God and a commitment to live as a disciple of Jesus Christ. Behold, all things can become new.

The Christian gospel and world-view offers great help for persons to redirect the sufferings of their lives into constructive channels. After all, God found a way to allow His Son's most awful, unjust sufferings to become the greatest blessing to the world. Your tactful summaries can help your counselees begin to catch glimpses of the ways in which God is ready to transform the sufferings of their lives into something redemptive.

12. *Suggest Parallel Readings and Homework*

A great deal of the insight, the setting free, the glimpsing of hope, the confession, repentance, and determination to change, and the selection of next steps to take does occur in the counseling hours, deep in the interpersonal relationship between yourself and your counselee. This is as it should be. The quality of the relationship between yourself and your counselee is very near to the essence of counseling. Do not try to manipulate your counselee by arrangements made behind his or her back, such as taking a spouse or boss aside and suggesting things they can do help your counselee.

But you can enrich the total process with certain of your counselees by pointing out carefully selected literature they can be reading between sessions. You can agree upon this as "homework" to read between sessions. Try to sense when your counselee is working on his or her problem at a factual and rational level and when at a deep emotional level.

Readings you suggest for your counselees should not be merely generalized literature of good advice, inspiration, and encouragement. They should not be success stories by "superior saints." This kind of literature will seldom contribute much to your counseling. Such literature tends to repeat what your counselees have heard often before. If it failed to help them to solve their problem before now, hearing the familiar material once more will not likely help much now.

Don't loan your counselees literature on a hit-or-miss basis. If you decide to loan literature, do so on a "diagnosis and prescription" basis. Know your literature so thoroughly and your counselee's need so well that you can make a reading assignment with the confidence of a good medical doctor prescribing medicine.

Good literature, carefully prescribed to fit a clearly discerned and diagnosed concern and need, can increase the help you offer your counselees. You can fortify a sense of direction ("in the multitude of counselors there is safety") and your counselees can gain increased certainty if some appropriate literature helps to shape their emerging decision.

Honor the real growth counselees often achieve between your sessions of counseling. Sometimes incubation and prayer can work marvels. Counselees often achieve a breakthrough in their problem when they begin working at it in an organized way, on specific issues, with workable next steps agreed upon.

Some counselees respond well to a behavioral contract which spells out just what steps will be taken—where, how often, when, with whom, and how long. If rewards for stick-to-itiveness are built into the contract, this also helps.

You will not likely find the "ready-made answers to common problems" sort of booklet or pamphlet very useful. They may read like an interesting "Dear Abby" or "Ann Landers" column when your counselees are feeling well and emotionally strong. But when they are hurting deeply and are profoundly perplexed, the generalized answer to somebody else's problem simply will not do. Often your counselees will be angered by simplistic answers. They sense that they are being given "Saul's armor" to fight with. The answer designed for someone else does not fit. They cannot use it. They may be alienated as a result of moralistic or literature or Bible prooftexts given when they are in deep distress. They will likely resent the saccharin-sweet, easy, pious reassurances of many popular pamphlets.

Literature like Paul Tournier's *The Meaning of Persons* may open windows for a counselee seeking his own personal identity. When a counselee is deeply discouraged by baffling and recurring defeat, James Mallory's *The Kink and I* may speak to his or her condition. If your counselee has experienced tragedy, E. S. Howland's *Speak Through the Earthquake* may help.

If your counselees are troubled by the inability to enjoy solitude, achieving instead only a painful loneliness, *Reaching Out* by Henri Nouwen may speak to their condition. If you are trying to help counselees who have fallen out of the love they fell into as adolescents, and are trying in mid-life to regain a mature love in their marriage, *The Art of Loving* by Eric Fromm may prove useful.

A counselee is not ready to terminate counseling until he or she can describe a plan of action in specific terms. Counselees cannot implement a plan of action if they are still too fuzzy about it to state it clearly. Counselees will not work hard at a given solution unless they take emotional ownership of it, and feel it is really theirs.

It helps some counselees to pick several models to emulate, persons they admire who are now succeeding in the attitudes and behavior the counselees want to reach. Model following is one more aid which may help some persons.

13. *Conclude the Session Carefully*

Next to the tact and skill with which you enter a counseling relationship and set a contract, no other part of your entire counseling process is more crucial, more potent for good or ill, than the way you go about terminating the counseling relationship with your counselees. Just as the termination of your life (and how you regard your own approaching death) can add meaning, depth, and intensity to your experience of life itself, so the way you plan to terminate a deep counseling relationship changes the meaning of each counseling session. If you are too lavish with support and reassurance, you may lead your counselee to terminate the relationship too early, before real insight and clarity of working plan have been achieved.

Some counselors ignore the powerful dynamics of termination by simply refusing to deal with it. They may try to keep the counselee "on call" to them indefinitely and thus dependent upon them. A dribbling on and on, unclarified relationship between counselor and counselee consumes time. It may feed the counselor's ego and need to be a god-figure. It may keep the counselee from mature independence. You and your counselee may unwittingly comprise a snug little clique within the congregation if you prolong your confidential covenant unduly long. Many counselors assure themselves of future "patients" and themselves of a future job by refusing to terminate with their counselees.

Some counselors admit, albeit under their breath, that they rely upon the pain of paying the fees to help the counselee to conclude that they really can go it alone (with the support of their regular group and friends). But you, as a fellow member of the congregation, will not be charging fees. You will not have the benefit of counselees determined to "get what I'm paying for" which fee-paying sometimes adds. But you will not have the fear that you are discriminating against the poor who cannot pay. You will not meet the deep resentment against having "to buy love for $30.00 an hour" which some counselees feel in a fee-paying relationship. And you will not have counselees terminating the relationship because they are out of money. All in all, it is an asset all the way through, and especially at termination time, not to charge fees. When, like the Apostle Paul, you support yourself with your own hands, your voice is the most free to serve as a counselor.

If counselees give their money to a pastoral counseling fund of their congregation, the act is a deeply religious act of worship, devotion, and gratitude. To merely buy services is a merchandizing act. It is good for both you and for your counselees if they do not pay you for your help.

Both you and your counselee should be aware you are moving toward terminating the relationship. Often a counselee will seek to delay this by bringing up some completely new material. You must recognize this for what it is.

If you renegotiate your contract periodically, then this can provide some "end setting." Ask your counselees to face up to just what more they are needing and wanting. If you tactfully bring up the matter of termination, your counselees will likely get down to business with new vigor. Usually they achieve a sharper focus after they sincerely ask, "What lack I yet? If we go on for more sessions, precisely what will we work on? How will I know when I have gained the insight needed so that counseling sessions should cease?" Sometimes you will terminate because the counselee is saying essentially, "I want help but not yet." But do not terminate if strength from your relationship is keeping your counselee intact.

You will need to discuss termination with great sensitivity if it is to bring the desired side effects. You dare not be disliking your counselees, bored with your counselees, despairing about them, or pretending they are "All-OK" because you really are at your wit's end on

how to help them. They will experience any of these attitudes as rejection however well you try to hide them. If
your counselees are not sufficiently okay you should refer
them, and not terminate just to get rid of them. You need
not continue counseling until your counselee is feeling
good, but until your counselee has insight into possible
solutions to the problem and is more courageous to work
hard at these solutions.

When you bring up the possibility and advisability of
termination, some counselees may react in anger, charging you with not caring. This provides you with real
agenda which was there all the time, and is merely
surfaced by talk of termination. If termination is done
tactfully, you are merely resetting the relationship into a
mutual friendship one. Structured counseling can be
begun again, but a new contract-covenant will need to be
agreed upon. After a tactful termination the privileged
communication ceases, mutual give-and-take is resumed,
but your friendship with these persons may possess an
extra warmth ever after.

At termination time you will be glad that you had no
"god-complex" when you began counseling. You did not
enter counseling with grandiose notions that you can
help all counselees with all kinds of problems. Your ob-
jectives were much more limited. You were aware always
that you needed to refer some of your counselees to
others because you could not seem to help them at all.
You were glad to help even a little. But many times just a
little help on a few problem areas of a counselee's life can
make the difference between victory and defeat. Your
goals may well be like those of the ancient inscription
over a hospital door in Paris: "To cure sometimes, to help
often, to comfort always."

14. *Avoid Unhelpful Responses*

Following are some responses of the kind to avoid. Avoid these verbal responses because of what they may imply to the counselee about his or her intelligence, freedom, and ability to decide wisely.

1. *Warning, threatening:* You had better . . . if you don't, I'll . . . consider the consequences . . . you'll be sorry if . . . beware that . . .

2. *Commanding, Ordering:* You must . . . you will . . . you have to . . . that's the law . . . I'm telling you to. . . .

3. *Obliging, Moralizing, Admonishing:* You should . . . you ought . . . it is your duty . . . please do it . . . I urge you . . . there is no other way. . . .

4. *Giving Answers, Solutions:* Why don't you . . . I suggest that . . . try this . . . have you thought of . . . the right way is . . . the truth is. . . .

5. *Arguing, Persuading, Instructing:* Yes, but . . . the facts are . . . you are wrong . . . most people do . . . you had better. . . .

6. *Judging, Evaluating, Blaming:* You are mistaken . . . don't you see that . . . it will be your fault . . . you know it isn't right. . . .

7. *Approving, Praising:* You've done a good job . . . I approve of . . . excellent . . . that is the way I do it, too . . . aren't you glad you. . . ?

8. *Reassuring, Excusing, Sympathizing:* Don't worry . . . it's not so bad . . . you are not to blame . . . you couldn't help it . . . everyone does it. . . .

9. *Interpreting, Psychoanalyzing:* What you really mean is . . . your motive is . . . I hear you saying . . . unconsciously you are trying to . . . your parent is talking now.

10. *Probing, Prying, Cross-Examining:* Why did you . . . now be honest . . . how . . . when . . . are you sure . . . what are you trying to hide. . . ?

Lest all of these warnings about responses you should never use leave you with a fear of trying to counsel at all, go back at this point and reread sections three, four, five, and six which stress the many helpful responses you can use.

4

VOCATIONAL COUNSELING

1. *Remember That Many Persons Offer Vocational Counseling*

Vocational choice is usually a happy crisis in life, or at least it can be and should be. Yet it is a crisis which calls for conferring and the receiving of counsel. Vocational changes will come for yourself as well as for others. You should be ready to receive counsel at such times, and to give it to your friends in the church.

Remember, when you counsel with young people about their choice of vocation, that you are only one among a number of counselors. Likely vocational counselors in high school have made suggestions. Often parents let their preferences be known in not too subtle ways. Peers bring their pressures of approval or of disapproval. The choice of a college major may hasten vocational choice.

Review with your counselees all that aptitude tests, interest inventories, and other such aids have already told them about their special abilities. Find out what coaches, peers, and fellow employees have offered in feedback. Inquire what kinds of work they have sampled. Attempt to learn what they have done which has given them the deepest sense of satisfaction and fulfillment.

Vocational counseling can be thoroughly enjoyable, and yet quite serious, and even sobering. Your counselees will not usually be secretive, nor have guilt feelings to hide. They may talk freely, but be groping for the deeper feelings they sense are emerging as they try to "open their sealed orders." Try to help your counselees explore their deeper feelings.

Encourage them to regard the choice of their vocation as a slow process, rather than as a once-for-all crisis. Suggest that they observe trends in their own lives. Decisions may be reached little-by-little.

2. *Be Understanding If Your Counselees Are Perplexed*
Your counselees may have read that few people are really happy in their work. They may be daunted by the long and expensive periods of training which many specialized vocations require. They may wonder which jobs will become obsolete because of continuing changes in technology and ecology. Persons facing vocational choice have a right to be perplexed.

You will need to be understanding if some youth feel reluctant to enter the "rat race." They may have witnessed the ulcers and up-tight existence of parents or relatives. They may secretly resent the tyranny of labor unions, the snobbishness of professional associations, or the boring monotony of assembly lines.

As counselor, listen with your third ear and read between the lines to sense whether your counselees really see any dignity in work. They may not have learned "to bear the yoke in youth" nor to appreciate the Protestant work ethic. They may actually idealize leisure and resent work. If they grew up unreflectively in a situation in which parents paid their children's way from birth to adulthood, your counselees may hope to work as little as possible and to loaf as much as possible. In that case your role as counselor is a deep and difficult one.

Your first task as counselor is to hear the level of questions your counselees are asking as they think about vocation. Their minds may hover only on the surface around questions of how much pay, with how many fringe benefits, with what promotion possibilities, with how healthful an environment, and with what class of fellow workers, and so on. You will need to take these questions seriously. And you will be concerned that your counselees find a job in which all of these are maximized. But underneath all this you will be hearing whether service to others is the goal or whether self-centeredness seems to be dominant. You will be noticing whether the person is really seeking first God's kingdom when choosing a vocation.

3. *As a Christian Counselor, Raise Special Concerns*

You may find yourself needing to "go against the

stream" of other counseling your counselees have been receiving. You cannot, in all good conscience, remain silent if you find that affluence and self-seeking have been accepted as goals. Some of your responses will need to be probing ones. At this point, even your counseling may need to be prophetic.

As a Christian counselor you will be concerned that any work a Christian does is seen as a part of the work God is seeking to do in and for His world. Your counselees may need your help to set their vocational choices into this larger context.

Encourage them to think about which human needs call most loudly for their aid, what causes are worth giving their lives to, and what challenges are so great and so crucial that they fill ordinary days with meaning.

You cannot honestly raise such questions with the tenderness, the sensitivity, and the seriousness which they deserve unless you are willing to enter into a deep growing relationship with your counselees. "Deep must be calling to deep" when such sacred issues are discussed. Your own "gates must be open" until your two psyches flow together, and you have the meeting of souls which Carl Jung has described.

If you and another Christian have met as in the presence of Christ, and your counselee is asking, "Lord, what will You have me to do?" this is churchly reality of a high order. You will have the sacred opportunity of searching together in a spirit akin to worship and prayer.

You will be concerned about any enabling gifts for ministry which God's Spirit may have given to your counselees, and which may have been identified and discerned by their church group. Your counselees will feel differently about their choice of a life work if they honestly believe that God and His people were directly involved in the discernment of their gifts and call. Vocational counseling can take on a whole new dimension of reality. <u>Your counselees can go to their daily work as if sent by God, if they feel God's Spirit has led throughout the process.</u> Your counseling should supplement and assist the admonition received from their church group, and never replace it.

If your own and your counselee's supreme vocation is to be a disciple of Christ, with daily work a channel to express that discipleship, this will rule out some jobs or vocations as unsuitable. Some jobs may be dropped from consideration by your counselees because of their side-effect upon ecology, because of bad effects upon family or health, or because of associates involved. No Christian should just "hunt-a-job" in the uncritical way it is often done.

You should help your counselees to detect God's providential leadings toward a vocation. As counselor you will listen deeply as they talk about vocational options and the movement of their feelings, as they weigh all the evidence and share any providential leadings they have sensed. You will suggest taking plenty of time. If they place service through the church high on their list of life's priorities, the implications for church fellowship and service will come up early in discussing a given job.

4. *Assist Your Counselees to Weigh Options Carefully*

What will you as counselor say to the assembly line option and the possibility of being suffocated with boredom? What if your counselees must exchange their time for money without knowing the usefulness of the thing they are making? Will you pass along the old-time lie that "hard, gruelling work makes heroes"? Counseling demands absolute honesty!

If your counselees are Christians of the all-too-rare kind who feel called by Christ to serve rather than to rule, to love enemies rather than to seek to destroy them, to suffer rather than to cause suffering, to give rather than to seek to accumulate, to live for eternity and eternal values rather than for fleeting enjoyments—then your counselees should deploy their lives carefully! The "law of parsimony" should apply. There are not enough of such persons to go around! They should choose their vocations strategically. They should serve in the crucial and focal positions where persons of their rare kind can do the most good. You as their counselor should help them to ponder prayerfully just where their Lord wants them to be positioned.

Even within Protestant churches, young people may be asking about remaining single and celibate in order to be more free to serve Christ. As counselor you will need to think through your own theology to be able to assist persons with this question or vision.

You will be concerned that your counselees do not merely choose a given vocation to copy their parents, nor avoid it merely to rebel against parental hopes. Your counselees' sense of values will become exposed as you discuss vocational choice. Principles of Christian stewardship will be involved. Attitudes toward work, toil, drudgery, leisure, and self-discipline will always crop out. As counselor you can help to keep the spotlight of your counselees' attention focused upon those issues which are crucial. You may find a kind of "permanent kid-hood" of irresponsibility or peevishness in some of your vocational-choice counselees. If so, move slowly.

5. *Seize Upon "Teachable Moments"*

Vocational counseling may come along with friendly chats you are having from time to time. Because no shame is associated with it, and little need for secrecy, you may find yourself doing vocational counseling during heart-to-heart talks. Your friends may ask for your advice, or for your opinion, or even for information.

If you discover that your counselees are still flippant, still functioning at an immature level of influencing and being influenced by others, dangle before them more mature considerations. If they are basically selfish and waiting for others to serve them, or are finding importance by their ability to say a defiant "no," or even if they feel important by dominating and controlling others, they will not likely be finding deep satisfaction in any vocation. If you can open for them the options of loving and serving others, of giving themselves to a great cause, you will be their truest friend and counselor. Some persons need simple teaching before they can make a meaningful vocational choice.

Be alert for "teachable moments" at all times during vocational counseling. You may need to raise crucial aspects of vocational choice which your counselees have not thought about at all. If you are counseling someone during the growth stage, before 14 years of age, keep your counsel quite tentative, allow a good deal of fantasy, and include some appropriate instruction. During the exploratory stage of 15 to 25 years, most of the issues raised earlier in this chapter can be pursued. If you are counseling a person who is already established in a given vocation in relation to a possible change, then still more issues need to come into focus. These will be discussed more fully under section 8.

6. *Respect Each Counselee's Uniqueness and Worth*

If you are counseling members of minority groups who are experiencing unfair discrimination, you dare not ignore these realities. Your own social conscience may become aroused as you counsel. Strength to cope with injustice without becoming tragically embittered—this may be what your counselee needs even more than a job. Some blacks insist that a quiet rage burns within them because of long discrimination.

Be careful not to imply that your counselees' worth as persons is equated with the salary they can earn. Try to help each counselee to claim his or her own core worth regardless of whether a particular counselee is slightly retarded and will always serve in lowly ways. If you deeply respect and value your counselees' uniqueness and dignity as persons, they will detect your attitude even though you never say so in words.

7. *Counsel Youth to Keep Their Vocational Choices Tentative Until Marriage*

Some youthful counselees may hope that their future marriage partner will be able to share in their vocational choice. Some vocations, such as medical doctor or pastor, are so demanding in schedule and energy output that marriage is inevitably effected. It seems only fair that a prospective husband or wife choose his or her role freely and not feel forced to accept the side-effects of a partner's vocation without having had a voice in the matter.

Obviously, the wife's profession or vocation, even outside the home, is just as important as the husband's. Couples are just beginning to accept this reality when either partner makes his or her vocational choice. You, as counselor, can help your counselees to face the new day in this matter.

Some young persons who "have their headlights on" and their eyes open to the new demands, if a good marriage is to be achieved, frankly offer to reconsider the vocation of each partner as a part of their marriage covenant and vows. Few professional women are satisfied anymore with the self-effacing cry of the woman of 2,500 years ago. "Whither thou goest, I will go; where thou lodgest, I will lodge: thy people shall be my people." Professional women are more likely to say, "If I am to be married to you, you will need to choose freely to 'meet me in the middle' and to share every major choice in full mutuality."

Persons choosing to remain single deserve to have this choice respected, but they still need help in making a decision about their life vocation.

8. *Recognize that Career Changes Also Call for Vocational Counseling*

Keep alert to the counseling help persons need when they consider changing careers in mid-life. Many persons will change professions or jobs several times during their lifetime. Somehow, their earliest work no longer seems focused to the most pressing human needs. Because of their own inner changes they feel they need to move on. They want to keep living in fidelity to their own inner uniqueness and to the changing call they are hearing from Christ. They may feel the appeal of adventure and of new frontiers.

As counselor, help them test their inner restlessness and desire for change. Are they perhaps running away from persons involved in their present job, rather than claiming God's grace to work the difficulties through to a reconciliation? Or, have they inadvertantly become a victim of the "Peter Principle" which asserts that persons sometimes are promoted to a level above their best and most comfortable ability to function effectively? Has the size of their present job outrun their gifts and capacities? Does something about it go contrary to their personal ethics?

If you are counseling a "workaholic" for whom work has become an addiction, what will your counseling goals be? What is your own functioning doctrine of work? Can you relate equally well to the tension-ridden worker, the three-ulcer person for whom work has become a compulsion, and to the "hippie-type" who prefers to stay out of the establishment altogether? Vocational counseling will test your breadth, patience, and tolerance, your grasp of human nature, and your ethics as profoundly as any counseling you do.

Search your own heart to determine whether you believe deeply and fundamentally that your counselees are free, that they are goal oriented, able to form goals and strive to reach them, and capable of actualizing their own truest potential. You dare not see them as helpless pawns, driven by their own past or by blind instincts. Your basic assumptions will guide and shape the way you respond. If you believe your counselees are made in God's image and possess an inalienable right to self-determination, you will not quickly be tempted to lapse into advice-giving or manipulation. Vocational counseling is growth counseling. It is hearing and responding to God's call and claim. It is saying, "Here am I. Send me."

As counselor keep in mind that massive social pressures in our society push your counselees toward conformity to the world. Few persons or groups invite and evoke counselees to explore and develop their own uniqueness and individuality. There are few to applaud the struggling inventor, the person who dares to be different, and the creative innovator. Keep reminding your counselees of their own unique personality, their own unique gifts, their personal sense of their own call, and their own solitary sense of dignity, duty, and destiny.

However, do not make vocation the measure of your counselees' worth. Be careful you do not totally define persons by what they do! Do not assume that what persons produce for society determine their value. Do not lead your counselees to measure personal worth by the yardstick of utility! Do not lead your counselees to conclude that they cannot find meaning in life unless gainfully employed!

Rather, help your counselees relate their vocation to their inner-self, their core worth, their true integrity as persons which will abide even after they have retired or have lost a vocational focus for their life. Help them see that even though vocation is crucial and important, it must be interpreted into a full life of worship, contemplation, prayer, and leisure. Help them find meaning in beauty, in experience, in meditation, in solitude, and even in suffering. Only then is vocation set in its truest and largest context!

Walk carefully with counselees considering a job change in mid-life as they think through the implications of the proposed new job. How much new training will be required and what will it cost? What mobility will be involved? What will be the implications for church loyalties and involvement? What effect will the change have upon family and upon lifestyle? What about the security and seniority they may be surrendering by the change?

Help your counselees to test carefully any plans to expand a present hobby into a new full-time vocation. Many times something which is exciting when done rarely and "just for fun" loses its appeal when it must be done daily to earn a living. (Oil painting can be a most creative hobby, but few can make it really pay!)

You might well encourage your middle-aged counselees who are considering a change of career to take again a battery of aptitude and personality tests. Help them examine the next stage in their life carefully to appraise the previously undeveloped potential which is even now pressing for use and expression. Applaud their adventurous faith if it becomes clear, after sustained investigation and prayer, that the person is indeed breaking free from a boxed in and unfulfilling life, and is moving toward a life of fuller service.

Counseling middle-aged persons who are considering significant vocational changes can be some of the most enjoyable counseling you will ever do. You can help them discuss their plans carefully with persons already in the new job they are contemplating. You can sense whether they find most fulfillment working directly with people or whether a latent creativity in working artistically with their hands is one of their unused gifts.

Even "retirement age," so harshly set by many professions and industries, should become a time for new career counseling. Your counselees who have reached the age of 65 may resent being placed on the shelf. Help them to locate areas of unfinished business in their lives. Help them to admit things they have always wanted to do, but have never yet tried. Draw out their feelings about attempting a period of Voluntary Service. Explore with them creative uses of leisure and the new possibilities inherent in a latent skill. Encourage them to keep investing in intergenerational activities, to write down some of the wisdom which life has taught them, and to find new frontiers and adventures for their own inner spirit.

5

PREMARITAL COUNSELING

1. *Temper the Romantic with Realism*

You will find yourself looking forward to your work with engaged couples as some of the most enjoyable counseling you do. If you are so fortunate as to be a member of a congregation in which the pastor refers such persons to you for four or six sessions, your enjoyment will be still greater. This is a congregation functioning at its best. You can have the joyous assurance that with careful counseling before marriage, less couples will turn up a few years later in the heartache of divorce. Comparing in your mind the gushy love letters many couples write to one another before marriage, with the bitter charges they hurl at one another before their divorce lawyers a few years later, should help you bring realism to your task. Beware of a romatic trip on "Cloud 9" as you counsel.

2. *Prepare Yourself for Premarital Counseling*

Do not accept premarital counselees referred to you, nor volunteer to counsel them, nor respond to their own request to you for counsel, unless you are willing to prepare yourself by advance reading on why marriages are failing. But look for material with substance. Few things are more dreary and irrelevant than some of the superficial and popular "advice to the newly married" columns, pamphlets, and sermons (unless it would be the movie romances and the innuendos in commercial advertising on what makes a happy marriage).

The counselees will usually come to you in an elated mood, happy that they are "getting" the one they love. They are likely to feel in a hurry to get married, with dates already set in their minds. Often they are being swept along in the romantic tides of sexual attraction. You may feel that the wag was right when he said, "Entering marriage is a game of blind man's bluff, only both parties are blinded!"

Don't try to assume a special counselor's role much different from your ordinary self. Your warm, honest, human self is what you have to share. Be sure you offer all you have and are, without reserve and without veneer. Don't try to force feelings you do not have. Don't retreat behind your helping role of counselor as a facade.

Don't pretend to have an illuminating understanding

122

of the other person or persons, if you are really confused and unsure about who they really are in their truest selves. The first questions they raise about their compatability for marriage may be just a decoy for deeper questions. Just give yourself to a true and deep relationship with them, and be reflecting upon the profoundest and truest insights you know about marriage realities. Keep listening and loving and caring with all that you have and are.

For your private devotions during the time you are counseling an engaged couple, meditate upon what God meant when He said that two persons can become one flesh. What is that mystical, sacred, deeply spiritual flowing together which two covenanted lovers can know during sexual union? What does the Creator mean when He infers that his divine image is expressed in this new creation, this new oneness, this marriage union? Consider what it means to leave every other love and loyalty, and to make every other devotion secondary so that two can cleave to one another, under God, in a permanent commitment and "until death do us part." How can a love be so exclusive of all others, so possessive and all enfolding, so passionately claiming and holding, and yet set the loved one free, free to follow his or her own unique pattern of becoming?

3. *Insist That Premarital Counseling Be Thorough*

Don't be fooled by the young couple who feel they know all about marriage because they know all about sex. Don't be put off by the couple who feel that they do not need counseling because they have "had therapy." Usually mental health professions have goals for their "patients" such as (1) absence of illness; (2) adaptive behavior; (3) ability to conform, and (4) competence. All these are good, but very minimal, and do not begin to replace penetrating premarital counseling.

You will be equally dissatisfied with engaged couples who feel that their marriage simply must succeed because they both "just know we are made for each other." You will seriously question the strength of the relationship of semi-strangers who "fell madly in love." You will be genuinely concerned when you find a partner feeling trapped into a marriage because the girl is pregnant.

Urge your premarital counselees to take time to ponder carefully the meaning of doubts one or both of them are having about marriage. A marriage consummated in spite of serious doubts is more likely to have trouble later on. As counselor you will be kept alert to doubts due to possessiveness, jealousy, quarreling, irritability, dislike of one another's friends, domineering, and giving and receiving criticism.

What will be your attitude and approach when asked to counsel interfaith and interracial marriages? You will do well to read up on the considerable body of good research findings available in this area. Help the couple explore what their own uniqueness means to them, how good they are at dialogue, and their openness toward their united future. Do they hold values deeply, or just from the outside as borrowed from their group, their race, their family, or their stereotype?

As in all premarital and marriage-problem counseling, notice how clear the self-identity and self-respect of each partner is, how great the possibilities of compatibility between them, how strong the factors both within and around them which could drive them apart, and how deep the commitment and the quality of the sharings which bind their hearts together.

If one or more of your counselees has undergone a deep "journey into self" by sustained therapy, observe carefully the effects this is having. Therapy often frees people for honest relationships, but therapy also leaves some persons on a perpetual "inner trip," with the self-centered feeling, "I know myself better than you do." Unfortunately personal therapy does not always give a person great skill and tact in relating to other persons.

If you as a counselor have been doing your homework by serious reading in the field, and if your own marriage (if you are married) is a model of a successful union which sets two spirits free, then you will have in mind some of the crucial areas which tend to make or to break marriage. These issues should be discussed in all serious-ness and frankness as part of premarital counseling. A bit of self-disclosure about costly lessons you have learned in maximizing your own marriage may be appropriate.

4. *Use a Growth Counseling Approach*

Later you may need to face this same couple again, when they come in desperation for marriage-problem counseling because their beautiful union is coming apart at the seams. Then you may need to start with, "What went wrong with the way you had planned to live together?" But now, in premarital counseling, you start with what is realistically possible. Discuss with the couple their ideas for the best possible marriage. De- V liberately use a growth approach. Don't merely try to forsee and prevent possible failure.

Keep looking for their strengths which they can build upon. Help them verbalize their hopes and ideals and lay realistic plans to reach them. Help them even now to deepen their communication about crucial issues. Prepare them, too, for the possibility that they may tend to grow apart after marriage.

If, in your premarital counseling, you should find a massive deficiency in one or both of the counselees in areas of security, self-esteem, the ability to make friends, to actualize plans, or to think and comprehend, then you should frankly suggest sustained "personal problem counseling" to work on those unmet needs. Marriages can hardly be healthy if a massive personal need is unmet. Once in a while a couple manages to keep grinding along because their two neuroses just happen to fit.

Recognize potential trouble ahead if you discover that your counselees have not yet demonstrated that they can care sacrifically for someone else even more than they care for their own selfish interests. Remind them that it is risky to enter the mutual demands of marriage without having matured enough to be able to give self-forgetful, sacrificial, outgoing caring to another person.

As counselor listen for the deep goals and values they hold in common, as well as any which will inevitably clash.

Without lecturing them on the hard facts that marriage demands—a legal contract, a heart's covenant, an economic commitment, a sexual exclusiveness, and a social accountability—listen carefully to determine whether they realize what they are getting into in all of these areas. Do they resent the marriage license as a mere "papering over" of their union? Do they shrink from making their heart's vow to one another a kind of love not shared with parents, siblings, peers, or pals? Do they gladly blend insurance policies, debts, savings, and plans for investing or giving? Do they intend to keep themselves true to one another sexually even though all society goes berserk with promiscuous adultery? Do they want to become Mr. and Mrs. to be so known by society, happy to form a permanent and responsible social unity? Do they have problems about any aspect of what marriage entails?

If you discover that your premarital counselees are only suffering their normal share of the anxieties so characteristic of our times—value-confusion, emptiness and loss of meaning, childish consciences, and "religious future shock"—help them identify these as areas needing attention in their life together. Growing toward certainty in these areas can be a creative quest which gives depth and meaning to their marriage. It will help them not to be tempted to rely upon mere sexual adventures and novelties or self-centered affluence to keep their inner marriage reality alive. Marriage partners who are searching for life's meanings, clarifying their values, choosing their long-range goals, and developing their mastery of their professions so as to serve mankind— these persons can be happy together, even while growing and maturing as separate and unique individuals.

5. *Help the Counselees Claim Strengths to Build Upon*

Draw out one partner's feelings about the strengths she feels she is bringing to the marriage, while the other partner listens, prepared to answer back what portent for happiness or conflict he can foresee. (Then reverse the roles.) Ask, "What strong relationships do you have going in your life now other than with your fiancée? What are you contributing? Do you have good relationships with your parents and your siblings?" Your counselee will likely not be good at "cleaving" to a marriage partner unless he or she has been successful at leaving father and mother lovingly to become an autonomous person. Too many youth try *cleaving* in marriage before they finished *leaving* their parents.

Invite one partner at a time to respond aloud, as honestly as possible, in the partner's presence, to the question, "What new skills are you gaining in relating to peers, work mates, roommates, parents, and the like so that the other person feels fulfilled, set free, and enriched by them?" Keep in mind that the proposed marriage cannot be a rich one unless each partner develops this skill.

Ask each partner to rethink and describe the last two serious decisions they made in their lives, what procedure they used, what variable they pondered, and how they followed through. Reflect back to both partners whether you as counselor can detect that they are sensing the growth possibilities in the making of decisions. Caution them against a hasty marriage if you discover that decision-making patterns of either partner are still seriously immature, ill-considered, impetuous, or unmindful of the welfare of others.

If you find either one of your counselees adroitly changing the topic to something less threatening, make a careful mental note of this. Bring the couple back to the threatening topic. Help them find why it is too risky to talk about. Express your concern about any change of topic used to escape honesty.

If either of your counselees rambles on in jumbled confusion, ask that person to sum up their position on the matter in not more than three sentences. Ask each partner to select one or two adjectives which best describe their emotions at the moment. You will help them gain clarity if you "stop the story" and ask for introspection.

Somewhere in your counseling sessions with engaged couples try to discover how each one has been able to cope with suffering, pain, loss, defeat, or any hurting crisis of their individual life. Do they learn through suffering? Do they know how to incorporate sorrow, betrayal, pain, death, or the suffering of innocents into a mature philosophy of life? If they have not met any such experiences then you are dealing with emotional innocents or, at best, adolescents, and you as counselor should not blithely assure them that you are sure they will do okay. They are preparing to take one another for better or for worse. They are promising to share peak experiences and to walk together through any "valley of the shadow of death." In all honesty you need to discuss with them what this means.

6. *Help Them Examine Their "Fighting Style"*

If your premarital counselees have really come to know one another and done some significant dialogue together, then they will certainly have discovered where their two sovereign egos collide. Invite them to examine a recent confrontation. Were they able to offer to each other caring love a mile deep in the relationship, a love they did not need to earn, a calm ocean depth of love while a storm raged on its surface? How deep was their love beneath their very real difference? Can they confront one another caringly? How quickly does their professed love turn to anger and retaliation?

Invite your counselees to rethink their mutual exhortations, searching for the amount of honesty which was there. Were real feelings owned and admitted to the other? Were deep feelings or beliefs smothered or held back so that their "beautiful love" would not be tested? If they are willing to confront one another honestly about a difference which really matters, and can do it there in your presence, reflect back to them what you observe that is wholesome and what, in your opinion, requires further homework. Were they able to "speak the truth in love"?

When counseling engaged couples, try to sense all the while the depth of their affinity and of understanding on matters of having children, dividing household chores, career plans for both spouses, family prayers, obligations in child rearing, and finances and property rights. You need not insist that they have all of these all worked out in a contract ready to sign. But the fairness with which they are working at these will be extremely crucial. Urge that they achieve consensus on many of these areas. How they both feel about "women's liberation" emphases will also be important.

7. *Help Them Face Memories Which Need Cleansing*

As counselor inform yourself on whether they have tried "just living together" as a trial run. There is no evidence that such clandestine arrangements really help pretest compatability. On the contrary there is evidence that such persons often lose trust in one another's fidelity and trustworthiness. As counselor keep alert for handicaps, damaged self-respect, guilt feelings, and disapproval from their families which such couples are experiencing. If such emotions are present they should be worked through before marriage if possible. Unless a couple works through these feelings they may achieve only "negative fidelity" to one another—that is, a faithfulness built upon guilt and fear of consequences.

If either partner has been divorced from a previous marriage, plan to meet with each partner alone to explore in depth how many residual feelings remain and how they hope to handle these in the new marriage. If a divorced partner has really learned through the tragedy, has genuinely repented and is growing in the faith, then that partner may be able to succeed in a new marriage. But if any divorced partner keeps laying all of the blame upon "that other awful person," and is unwilling to take ownership of his or her real share of the failure, then such a divorced person is in no way ready for remarriage.

As counselor observe how either partner jokes about the other. All too often this subtle matter becomes a heavy weight upon the freely flowing feelings within a marriage. If you detect that one partner makes the other the butt of jokes, draw out that partner's true feelings about it. Too often the joke in public is a "safe" outlet for real guilts and feelings which are kept hidden while together at home.

8. *Help Them Develop Many Bases of Intimacy*

One of the best things you can share with counselees during premarital counseling is a mature and realistic view of the marriage relationship—the continuous readjustments, the ever new realignments, the never-ending adventure which successful marriage must be as two free persons, each growing in faithfulness to their own uniqueness, manage to stay close enough for their communication and mutual love to stay deep and real. You will be their truest helper toward a successful marriage if you give them a real taste of the good experience it is to seek for deeper intimacy with a partner.

Encourage your counselees to keep working for new intellectual, aesthetic, and creative intimacies. To know intimacy in one's intellectual life means to enjoy sharing mind-stretching discussions, to ponder together about things which matter profoundly, and to let minds roam together through great ideas. Aesthetic intimacy is reveling together in the enjoyment of beauty. Any marriage will be richer if both spouses can share some common tastes in architecture, artwork, sunsets, flowers, or music. Marriage is enriched when two hearts respond in common to beautiful scenes, people, landscapes, poems, or incidents.

Hold before your counselees the possibility of further intimacies in sharing some common recreation. They will find joy in one another if they can complete some creative projects together, can worship and pray together, and can both commit themselves deeply to a common cause. Sexual intimacy can become the icing on the cake, the joyous celebration of an intimacy already achieved in many other areas. It can symbolize and help to enrich a search for total union. It can become almost a fusion, a flowing together in joy and rapture.

Inform your counselees, lest the half-truths so common in our culture deceive them, that no sexual intimacy can long remain satisfying at the deepest level unless the other intimacies are happening. Unless two spouses are growing in oneness in many areas of their lives, mere sex experience seems to become as lonely and self-defeating an experience as masturbation. Young people may not yet know enough about life so that they can refuse the half-truths about sex which abound in the advertising and entertainment media unless you as counselor seize a few teachable moments to share this wisdom with them.

132

As a counselor keep in mind that money has a wide range of meanings in the lives of different persons. How do your counselees feel about the rich and the poor, about debts and savings, materialism, affluence, stewardship of money, and about a simple lifestyle?

Help your counselees <u>explore together their feelings about</u> school <u>debts</u> either one brings to the marriage, about charge accounts, a mutual savings plan, plans for tithing, filling out tax forms, <u>and accountability to one another for spending money</u>. If either partner has strong privacy needs about money, strong feelings about fairness or being cheated, about living from hand to mouth as compared with being well covered by insurance, help them to own and compare their deepest feelings in this area.

9. *Help Them Admit the Things That Bug Them*

If you discover that either or both of your counselees have quite a few strong dislikes, be sure to examine these. <u>Just what are the strong dislikes.</u> What common denominators appear among them? What is it that evokes the dislike? How is each partner coping with things or persons for whom they feel dislike?

Prejudices dealing with politics, race, health habits, religion, or ethics should be thoughtfully explored. Beware if there are meaningful issues which the engaged couple cannot discuss comfortably.

Encourage your premarital counselees to develop sensitivities regarding their own little accumulated oddities and idiosyncracies which bug their partner. The most absurd little quirks can become the tremendous trifles around which irritations gather, later to harden into dislike, and finally to fester into revulsion. See whether your couple can be tactfully, tenderly honest with one another about "the little things you do that turn me off." As counselor, <u>observe their patterns of honesty</u> or partial honesty, their defensiveness or openness, whether the things which bug the partner are deeply rooted in their spouse's upbringing. If you can help them not to sneer at tremendous trifles, not to treat lightly their partners preferences and habits about eating, cleanliness, grooming, sex, or social courtesies—then you will be helping them toward a happy and mutually considerate marriage.

10. *Help Them Relate Well to In-Laws*

Listen intently to learn how each future spouse feels about approvals, partial approvals, or disapprovals of their future in-laws. <u>Probe deeply into their expectancies of visits from in-laws, interventions by in-laws, subtle pressures from in-laws, or feelings of resentment toward in-laws.</u> Few newly married persons learn soon enough that while each partner can freely criticize his or her own parents, it hurts to hear the same words from one's partner. If the newlyweds plan to be dependent in any way upon either of their in-laws, the implications demand serious discussion. Each partner in a marriage really needs to leave father and mother.

If, however, your counselees intend to prevent all in-law problems by isolating themselves totally from both of their families, then you can foresee their loss of extended-family support which their emotional natures will need very much. Caution them against the myth that a solitary nuclear family, carefully cut off from relatives and roots, can achieve either personal identity or a low level of conflict. Help them find a realistic style of drawing upon the emotional strengths of their own clan while avoiding the interventions which can cause trouble.

11. *Help Them Test Whether They Really Like the One They Feel They Love*

In our culture the word "love" has come to mean conquest of a female by a male, with the female surrendering to the male's conquest. Rituals of male conquest linger in male initiative in dating, vocational choice, proposing marriage, accepting the bride from the arms of her father, carrying the captured bride across the threshold, promising to feed her, giving her the name of the male, initiating sex, and protecting her while she bears and nurtures the babies. Under this all-pervasive myth, love is an irrational swoon reaction that comes from nowhere and seizes the mind so that the person is helpless in its grip. Love is something to "fall into," made up of desire and dominance-submission, of conquest and capture. If the romantic swoon-feeling fades, then the person falls out of love again, obtains a divorce, and looks around for new conquest, seizure, and submission. No wonder self-respecting women are challenging the whole myth. A few faltering and confused voices are still suggesting that the captured woman can recapture her straying husband by being a seductive mistress, a "total woman" sexually. But the whole mythology of capture is wrong!

Help your counselees explore how much they deeply like their partner. Do they really admire and respect one another when each one is "doing their own thing"? Is companionship mutually satisfying, for its own sake, and not merely a price to be paid for the sex desired later on? Are your counselees able to create new sharing patterns which meet the needs of both? Can the couple share long-range planning so that they need not snatch at every pleasure now? Can they affirm one another's roots and hopes, so each can grow without diminishing their partner?

12. *Help Them Plan Vows They Really Mean*

During the final sessions of your premarital counseling, help your counselees write their marriage vows and covenant. Your own inner attitude of reverence for vows will be crucial. If you regard vows with awe and deep seriousness, so that in them you lay your whole life of trustworthiness and integrity on the line, then you will communicate some of these vibes to your counselees. Some marriage counselors with decades of experience are concluding that the place to start to prevent marital disasters is to help couples premediate their vows and promises reverently, until they mean every word of them deeply and identify their very self-respect with a determined intention to live true to them. Your counselees should be grasping the glad prospect that they will never need to fight or to forgive the same person twice, since both will always be growing, maturing, and becoming a still more interesting person to know.

If your counselees have grasped the importance of securing a "10,000-mile checkup," and of periodic efforts toward marriage enrichment, they would do well to include this in their promises to one another. You can help them exclude from their wedding that which is foolish, faddish, and sentimental, the suggestive signs, and all that is silly.

If they want to allow their marriage to "breathe," to keep some spaces in their togetherness so that each is free to grow, it might be well for them to say so as they begin their life together. Unless each knows solitude at times, and enjoys it, the partners likely cannot enrich each other fully when together. They could well promise each other to respect one another's "free space" and autonomy.

If they wish to keep some realistic kinds of romance in their marriage, but intend to go beyond romance to self-sacrifice and costly devotion for one another, they might do well to think through what they want to be saying.

If they hope to invite one another into the most sacred and secret aspirations they previously reserved for their private prayer closet, they might do well to work together to create their wedding prayer. The official who marries them may read other beautiful prayers, but their own prayer, prayed together as part of their wedding service of worship, may become a deep and tender tie that binds.

13. *Help Them Vow to "Meet in the Middle" Always*

Insist upon the Apostle Paul's foundational principle, "Be subject to one another out of reverence for Christ." Marriage must be 50-50, although to achieve that result, each partner will usually feel he or she is going 60 or 65 percent of the way so as to meet in the middle!

In a wholesome marriage there can be no boss and servant. There dare be no hints of superiority and inferiority. No one should need to feel dominated and reduced to subjection to the partner. When two strong persons marry, dominance tends to be shared about equally over the long run. Even if the home makes a great show outwardly that "the man is the head of his home," and even if the man boasts that "the buck stops here," or "I make the final decisions," inevitably the strong woman finds her way to balance out the dominance. If you are a wise counselor, you will begin with this assumption and will help the couple deliberately plan to be subject one to another. Only so can manipulation be minimized.

√ Help them scrutinize their discussion and decision makings about <u>choice of neighborhood, housing, furniture, and lifestyle.</u> Help them to meet-in-the-middle, being willing to compromise rather than either partner forging through to his or her own way. In a meeting-in-the-middle marriage the man must be able to keep saying also, "Where thou lodgest, I will lodge: thy people shall be my people, and thy God my God."

You can help to launch the couple upon their lifetime of mutuality if you give them a personal and emotional √ maturity test. Have each one rate the other partner, and then himself or herself. Have them covenant to use their greater maturity to help their partner to grow toward maturity. Help them to think of their lives as a good duet in which each tone is unique but moves always so that the result is harmony and not discord.

You can listen in, during premarital counseling sessions, as they review their decisions and tentative decisions about <u>type of friends, shared recreations, and hobbies.</u> You can hold before them the "meet-me-in-the-middle" ideal, as one gives in more here and the partner gives in more there. The middle point at which they meet may vary, but the final average must be 50-50.

Your counseling tact and skills will be taxed to the utmost when you help the couple uncover and face honestly differences they cherish in religious practices, the types of worship services they enjoy, the dogmas they either appreciate or resent, the piety, programs, or

138

preachers they either like or can't stand, or art which evokes differing responses within them. Meeting in the middle may lead to relating to a third denomination than to either his church or her church.

If during premarital counseling you can help them to see the absolute importance of giving 50-50 to one another in mutual respect and tolerance, mutual prizing and honoring, mutual cherishing and yielding, then you can help them to incorporate this principle as part of their marriage vow. All the rest of their days together throughout their married life they will need to meet-in-the-middle in their readiness to risk, to trust, to forgive, to be reconciled, and to begin again. All their married life each partner will need to keep repenting from any self-centeredness which would benefit one at the expense of the other. Help them adopt as a vow and motto of their marriage the mutual plea, "Always meet me in the middle."

6

MARRIAGE PROBLEM COUNSELING

1. *Expect All Marriages to Have Problems*

Even when you are counseling single adults, one of their problems will be the "couple's world." Almost every other kind of counseling you do also involves some problem in family living. If you are counseling a bereaved person, a family adjustment is imperative. If a breadwinner is changing vocation, a problem may be created for the family. If a retarded child has been born or is being reared, family problems may result. During a serious illness, the family experiences crisis. Terminal illness and death involve the family deeply. Mental illness, divorce, promotions, anniversaries, alcoholism, retirement, all affect the family. Find out during your initial interview where else they have been going for help and what strong influences are impinging upon the person and family.

Expect that each partner in the marriage will identify the problem differently. Disbelieve any report that "it's all his fault" or "it's all her fault." Almost always there is failure on both sides. You can expect clusters of problems, all interrelated. Trying to lift out one problem is like serving yourself from a dish of spaghetti. The whole dishful wants to come along!

2. *Approach the Marriage as a Whole, a System*

You will be wise to consider the marriage as a whole, as a relationship, or as a "system." When there is a marriage problem, the system is out of balance. Both spouses and the children (if there are any) are involved. Any change in one partner upsets the system by just that much. Seldom can you really help a marriage by counseling with only one partner. You will find, however, that usually the wife will come for counseling first, bringing her husband along reluctantly. He will be willing to come if it is for "the marriage," since he does not see this as a threat to him directly.

You have the priceless advantage of being able to go to their home, to see them in their family situation, to feel the atmosphere which is either nourishing, chilling, or destroying them. In recent years others who are doing marriage counseling are learning the old-fashioned virtue of making house calls again. Some of your counseling should be away from their home too, on neutral turf, possibly in a church parlor reserved for that hour. But keep the whole family in mind as you counsel with one member of a marriage.

No matter how thoroughly you did your premarital counseling with a couple, if they return five or ten years later, you are likely to find a host of problems neither you nor they could have foreseen. Each of the marriage partners has been developing and changing, trying to actualize their own inner potential, but they have been growing apart. There is less to talk about. Times they do have together are less satisfying. They may be disillusioned and almost hopeless. Or one may have done something rash which has forced open the whole mysterious problem.

3. *Understand the Feelings of the Wife*

If you have been doing your background reading on what is causing conflict in a multitude of married couples, you are alert to the problem of the unfulfilled mother. Often she was educated for something other than housekeeping, yet is spending her prime years at it. You hear her talking of her profession "passing her by," of losing seniority in it, and self-confidence as a person. You notice that she is taking her pulse for the happiness she is entitled to, and admitting that she feels angry and almost betrayed. Either she sweeps the floors and does the laundry with a listless boredom, or else she makes rearing her children into an overly-intense and full-time occupation. She may have tried to be everything to everyone by being sexy with her husband, a chauffeur to her kids, and a volunteer worker for myriad agencies. If she has listened to popularized psychoanalysis she hears that all she can expect for her efforts is to become the oppressive, ugly parent of her children's imagination, and a hindrance if they are ever to really become adults.

You will be wise to find out who she has been listening to or taking counsel with. If she has been reading radical woman's lib literature she will seek one set of solutions. If she has been listening to TV cosmetic commercials and soap operas, and reading "Can this marriage be saved?" articles in the popular journals, she may be seeking different ones. If she has been tuned to male chauvinism under a religious guise, she will have still different expectations.

4. *Listen Deeply to the Husband*

You will have to listen still harder to hear the feelings of the husband. He has been taught to suppress his tender feelings. If he is told his marriage is failing he takes this as a massive insult and personal threat to his ego. He thought his role was to be the provider, but all he can earn is gobbled up with little thanks and there is never enough. He may have had mingled feelings about his wife needing to earn, but periodically she must quit that to bear their children. Their children then compete with him for his wife's attention and affection. He may feel like a shuffler of meaningless papers or a tightener of endless belts all day long on the job. He comes home exhausted, hoping for a haven of love and rest, only to meet a blast of wifely frustration. She may expect him to become "mamma's little helper." She wants him to discipline the children but warns him not to damage their little egos. He knows that he is a poor model for the young males in his home with his feelings of being demoted, uncertain of his authority or role, absent, preoccupied, and tired.

The circle is a vicious one, endless and almost hopeless. Other equally anxious men he lives with at work escape into the dream world of sexy talk and jokes, or into the equally unfulfilling dream world of drink. At another economic level he may try affluence, travel, excitement, or extramarital affairs.

Whatever tender, unverbalized hopes the husband and father may have held that somehow he can correct his own impoverished past by helping his children to enjoy what he never had, the kids take as their right and are seldom grateful. If he wants to vicariously relive his own childish discoveries, joys, and wonderment it doesn't seem to work out. If he dimly hopes that his own flesh and blood will outlive him, and give him some perpetuity and permanance, he cannot say this out loud or claim it for sure. He vaguely knows he will die 7 or 8 years younger than his wife will and he doesn't even know what is killing him! And there is absolutely no circle of honesty in either job, lodge, club, or church where he can talk out these major anxieties of his life! If he hears boisterous claims that "man is the head," it makes him sick at heart.

You often can help your counselees if you hold up a mirror for them and help them see the two conflicting sets of feelings they are having. Beware, however, of getting into a rut as you reflect back their ambivalence to them so that you begin every response with "you feel, you feel, you feel." This is slavish adherence to a style, and will likely annoy your counselees.

5. *Involve Both Partners*
Some counseling centers have been content to try to save a marriage by working with one partner, but results

from such efforts are disappointing. Marriage partners tend to move farther apart if one partner goes to one counselor and the other partner goes to a different one.

Usually the wife will come first for counseling, reporting that her husband refuses to join her in counseling. Sometimes he will want to take counsel from his cronies, from friends he trusts, but most often he refuses it altogether. The modern male ego seems greatly threatened to have to admit, "I need help." Usually the man resents having anyone learn the secrets of their married life. One important reason to counsel with both partners is that there are always two sides to the problem, and one alone cannot solve the mutual problem. Real progress remains well-nigh hopeless if either party has given up on the marriage.

You should frankly call the absent partner, if he or she will not come in on the invitation relayed through the spouse. State candidly what you intend to do, give your pledge to absolute fairness and neutrality, and offer an appointment. Some loyalty seems to make men come in even if they have already secretly given up on their marriage.

Sometimes a partner who will not join in counseling will nonetheless be willing to fill out an evaluation form on the level of trust, communication, fairness, common interest, and the like in the marriage. By sending the absent partner copies of materials you are using, you can sometimes gain his or her trust until they will come in.

During the beginning phases of marriage problem counseling you may alternate seeing each partner alone until you are sure you can see both sides fairly and until each partner feels they can be honest in a face-to-face meeting.

You, as counselor, do not yet have the "feel" of the problem of your counselees until you can answer, at least to yourself, why the couple married in the first place, when problems developed, to whom else they have talked, what each one thinks the central problem is, how seriously they are thinking of divorce, what good still remains in the marriage, what part sex adjustment plays, whether there has been infidelity and a third party, and how much determination there is to work through to a solution.

Notice carefully the emotional attitude each partner has toward the emphases of the woman's lib movement. Their differing attitudes will likely come out if you ask them to discuss changing their roles in the home periodically, or woman's right to equal pay and executive positions, and abortion upon her own demand. Their divergent attitudes may come out as they attempt to discuss sexism in advertising, the ordination of women, or fairness in the divorce laws. If either he or she becomes emotional about the need for a female person in the Godhead, or the fact that job vacancies tend to mention sex, observe the amount of anger or disrespect they feel toward each other. Woman's lib issues help to surface how they feel about one another.

A similar movement toward male liberation is equally needed but was not as far advanced in 1977 when I was writing this book. But keep listening deeply to detect whether the man is liberated from his need to prove himself, from worrying about his "manly" appearance, and his status symbols in society. Is he free from a need to be in control, to have an answer at all times, to be the sole breadwinner and the expert? Is he free from any need to dominate? Can he really listen? Can he be intui-

147

tive as well as logical and intellectual? Can he express his true emotions or is he emotionally constipated? Can he value the spiritual quest of the women around him or does he see them mostly as sex objects?

How does the man feel about admitting the "feminine parts" of himself? Can he rejoice in his wife's success even in areas where they have been competing and in which she is now surpassing him? Is he willing to keep working, in relaxed fashion, for his wife's liberation equally with his own liberation, from the imprisoning stereotypes of the surrounding culture? What does he think is causing men in our society to die eight years younger than women do? The maturity, honesty, and balance with which the man can reflect upon these issues will reveal whether he is beginning to become a liberated person. If his wife can join him comfortably, she too is being truly liberated.

6. *Be Alert for Low Self-Esteem*

As you examine a family system, expect to find any number of little "holy wars" going on. One parent may be saying to the child, "Don't go near the water," while the other one is saying in effect, "Here's your swimsuit." Inconsistent rules may really be parental jabs at one another. At a deep level a mother is tempted to feel that her male children will line up with her husband against her in the hourly tit-for-tat and power struggles which go on in most marriages. Husbands seem to have the parallel fears. Somehow a great many interactions become competitive. Almost everything becomes an "I win—you lose" affair.

You will notice many times that a wife's self-esteem is threatened by lack of sincere appreciation for the endless little tasks that make up her days. She is unpaid at home and paid less than a man at the shop. As counselor you will find that each partner's problem with low self-esteem (and nearly everyone seems to have some problem here) is projected outward upon the marriage and often upon the children. A mother with a weight problem may allow it to lower her self-esteem and from her lessened self-respect lash out against her dieting or overweight daughter, her husband's eating habits, his lack of attention and tenderness, or his uncouth ways of engaging in sex. A husband with a boredom problem at the shop, a futility feeling in his profession, and who thinks he is being betrayed by his teenage children will interiorize a profound feeling of failure and worthlessness, of being a nobody.

Many times you will find the husband with a problem of low self-esteem clamming up, walking off, working late at the office, succumbing to alcohol or to a female seducer. Intermittently he may explode in anger, resort to force and threats, or enlist the children on his side. When the perennial problem of low self-esteem appears, keep watching for new sources of strength in the insecure persons. Reflect back to them resources they seem to have in a skill they have never fully developed, a character trait like courage which they can develop further, or a creative imagination they can focus upon solving their present problem.

If either partner refuses to look into your eyes, this may indicate that they are afraid of self-discovery. You may mention your surprise about this and try to make your own eye-contact comfortable, easy, inviting. If your own eye contact is domineering, boring, or tends to stare the other person down, you make honest eye-to-eye meeting harder and erect a barrier.

Your counselee's relationship with you may be characteristic of their relationship with other people. If you find yourself being repelled by a barrage of words, coyness, demure dishonesty, or by swagger, you may assume others do too. You are doing one of your greatest services to your counselees when you simply relate to them honestly and then tactfully tell them how you experience them. You are modeling what a real friend can be.

Sometimes you will notice that a low and muffled voice shows low self-esteem. Sometimes averted eyes, slumped shoulders, beseeching or cringing demeanor, or a hand held before the face reveal the person's desire to hide away. Be sure that you are actually imputing worth to the person, affirming subverbally, "I love you, I love you, I love you," if indeed and in truth you do.

7. *Sense If Religion Is a Real Strength to Them*

As a counselor who is consciously seeking fully to utilize your Christian world-view and assumptions, you will naturally be observing whether your counselees' faith is a liability or an asset to them in solving their problems. If their religion has given them a perverted view of God's good gift of sexuality, then they may not know how to utilize sex as their Creator intended. Instead of sex functioning to enrich relationships, create children, and renew the covenant of marriage, it may come out abortively as masturbation, homosexuality, uncontrolled fantasies, or prostitution. Their inner life may be ridden with taboos, guilts, uncontrolled desires, and impulses merely to use others as sex objects.

Religion can be either the greatest asset in releasing the creative powers of sexuality within the person or one of the greatest hindrances to good sexual adjustment. As counselor, explore how their religion forms or deforms their consciences. If their consciences need reeducating move very slowly and reverently, helping your counselees to take new soundings in the sources of their faith—in the Scriptures, prayer, sacraments, and church fellowship. If counseling women nurtured in legalistic backgrounds, you will need to move reverently as they rethink their choice of a mate, of contraception, or of sex as an experience of joy and ecstasy.

As counselor keep asking yourself whether your counselees have really internalized their religious values so that their ethical choices are made from inner consistency and conviction, or merely from external taboos. Watch whether counselees decide with adult two-sided maturity or from childish self-centeredness, merely using religion to support their immaturity. Notice whether your counselees use religion as a magical wand, a quickie answer, an instant solution which absolves them from personal responsibility or painful growth.

Sometimes you can help a couple stop a downward spiral if they pledge with you to pray aloud for one another every day. Conversational prayer, if simple and honest, can be a heart-to-heart sharing which refreshes the spirits and increases the optimism of marriage partners. If they have enough perceptive self-awareness to sense that their problem is related to unclarity of roles, to aggressive or dependency needs, to giving one another mutual respect and trust, then these needs are easier to work at if they are brought out into the open in tender, affectionate prayer.

You may find that during the early sessions of counseling troubled persons that they are rigid, out of touch with

151

their honest feelings. Then they begin to own and describe feelings they held long ago. At first when they dare to admit present feelings they may talk about them as an object out there, to be looked at objectively like a sore toe. If they can begin to own, describe, and accept feelings immediately present they are almost finished with their inner homework. When they have become comfortable with the full flow of their own inner experiencing, aware of and in control of the whole range of their inner emotions, then they should be able to cope with a wide range of either aggravating or pleasuring persons or events.

After your counselees are convinced you love them regardless of what they do, and after they believe you really help them to a free decision, they may invite you to be a collaborator in solving their problem.

8. *Help Them Find Handles to Solve Their Problems*

In marriage problem counseling always try to suggest one or two handles your counselees can take hold of to begin to upgrade their marriage. Several hours of loving listening will often reveal seven or even ten serious angles to their problem. They may recite them in rehearsed fashion until you feel overwhelmed. Should you begin with their financial crisis, their health problem, their unforgiven hurts, their religious deadness, their sexual frigidity, their fighting style, their in-laws muddle, or their concern for a delinquent teenager? Often they will mention troubles with their schools, jobs, schedules, and neighbors. Try to sense which of these are at the center of the logjam, the key to the whole system of trouble.

Keep in mind that they are counselees, and not patients. Keep them carrying the responsibility as much as possible. Don't let them seduce you into "playing doctor" and treating them as if they were sick. Don't allow them to keep looking to you for the magic pill, the miracle drug, which will heal their sickness and give them therapy. Whenever possible, reflect back to them the medley of problems you are hearing that they are having. Then ask them to choose the two (or three at the most) upon which they want to focus attention in this particular counseling situation. Assure them that if a couple who still care for each other and want to preserve their marriage can make real progress on just two or three of their problems they will be able to find new hope for working on all of the rest. Help them think through and plan wise action on one or two key aspects to their problem rather than touching lightly on a host of problems. Collaborate with them in selecting and working through problems.

You may even introduce them to the notion of "stress factors" in their marriage. If "normal" people can stand a stress load of about 30, and the death of a family member is rated about 6, a pregnancy 4, a severe injury 5, being fired 4, an illness 5, a separation 6, a mortgage foreclosure 3, and a change of residence 2, you can help your counselees to understand why their circuits are overloaded. Help them reduce their load of high stress factors and postpone new ones when possible to help them cope better now. Your task as counselor is often to help your counselees to admit their limits, to pace themselves, to tackle one problem at a time, and to be able to "get above and look down upon their problem" with just a bit of humor.

If one of the stress factors is just now painfully real to you, admit it honestly. Don't ask them to help you, but let them know that you are human too and know how it feels. Even though you share in your counselee's weakness, you are coping.

If you can't see a handle to their problem, admit this honestly, but show that you can persevere and keep trying. You might admit, "I don't honestly know what would be best for you to do. I wish I did." Just the fact that you really understand their feelings, and can verbalize them better than they can themselves, will be a tremendous source of hope to them.

9. *Help Them Improve Their "Fighting Style"*

Observe their ways of handling disagreements as you try to referee heated discussions between them. Rarely will they feel proud of the patterns they have drifted into, but left alone they seem powerless to change them. Little by little the need to win has overcome their desire to be fair and tactful. In order to win they have learned to attack one another's most vulnerable point. Overstatement may have become habitual. Words like "you never" or "you always" are blanket accusations which hurt and do not help toward compromise. If their unfairness is making you angry, admit it and process it then and there. They need a living demonstration that anger can be processed clearly, honestly, without destroying anyone, but can help truth to come through.

You will see married couples treating their most dearly loved partner with discourtesy they would not show to a stranger. You will see little games being played and manipulation. As you listen to implied threats notice that they are not really listening to one another but are scrounging in their arsenal of memories to unleash a rebuttal ready as soon as their mate quits.

If you have earned the trust of both partners that you are able to be fair and impartial, you can listen awhile, then feed back to them what you have been observing. See whether both can take ownership of elements of name-calling, stereotyping, exaggerating, blaming, or threatening which each has been doing.

You may find that they need help in hearing one another's meanings. Repeating back a spouse's meaning in other words is a good test of shared meaning. You can help them at first if you will summarize their progress and claim their common ground gained.

Occasionally you will have a couple in marriage problem counseling who "absolutely never fights." They never clash openly, but practice denial, sulking, little games of pressure and resentment. Soon such couples lose interest in one another, their sex life grows cold, and they find less and less to talk about.

You may observe deeper meanings to their squabbles as you come to understand them better. Some women scare up a squabble in the evening so they can avoid requests for intercourse later on. Some men must win a little argument at home because they just lost a big one with the boss at the shop.

In your refereeing of their arguments, help them upgrade their style for the future by challenging their archaeology (the digging up of stuff long past). Help them to avoid emotionally loaded words, to go easy around places their partner is hurting, to focus upon one problem at a time, to take ownership of part of the problem, and to refrain from psyching out their partner by decreeing "why" they do a certain thing.

Encourage their first timid moves toward forgiveness and reconciliation. Point out the deep caring you can sense beneath the disagreement. Sometimes a little tact-ful humor will lighten the mood and help quarreling partners to "catch-themselves-at-it" in some pretty ab-surd conduct.

After you are sure your counselees have gained new skills in disagreeing agreeably and in solving problems peaceably, help them to try to get in touch with the threat they were feeling. Affirm and encourage them in positive plans they have laid to improve their problem solving.

As you counsel your peers in the church, especially re-garding problems in their marriage, you are likely to find that some are staying together, plodding along in a joy-less marriage "for the sake of the children." Others stay together because "separation and divorce are sin," be-cause "we would be ashamed to have our friends know," because "our mutual friends want us to stay together," and so on. All these are useful secondary reasons to keep living with a spouse, but dare not become the primary reasons for doing so. The basic reason must always be that the deepest personal satisfaction lies in fulfilling vows, in conquering obstacles, in exploring new frontiers, and in maturing together as each one grows individually.

10. *Celebrate the Ground They Have Gained*

When you detect that your counselees can share without surrendering, point this out to them. If you sense that they have given up an unrealistic attempt to be all things to each other, call attention to this gain. If either one becomes aware that escape fantasies are lessening, celebrate this. If either is more comfortable to admit to a weakness and to ask for help, if either or both can give love as well as receive it, if either or both can prize the contribution the partner is making as highly as their own, if either or both are gaining in hopeful dreams for their future, if they are willing to work and watch and wait for the fruits of their love—celebrate these gains by calling attention to them.

You may want to pray with them, focusing intensely upon the future which you believe is possible for them. If they are anchoring their lives and hopes in a new plan they have formed for their future, if sex union begins to partake of deeper mystical and spiritual qualities, and if they are finding their union more nearly total, you will do well to claim it, seal it by thankful prayer, and solemnize it in a rewritten covenant. Partners depersonalize their love if it does not also have in it a plan for one another's welfare in the weeks ahead.

As part of being "honest you" totally present and with them, you may want to show the affection you really feel. Tell them you love them and that you are proud of them. If they are the hugging kind, have a threesome bear hug.

Just to "kiss and make up" or to "quit fighting for the sake of the kids" will not last. If their solutions were made in freedom on the part of both, with autonomous action, feeling with each other all the while—then it will likely last. If, from it all, they have become more creative in working at problems, more flexible in finding solutions, with a greater degree of mutual trust, then your counseling has indeed been successful. Try as counselor to leave them without any labels or psychological jargon they can use against one another if and when the next disagreement comes. Help them claim the joy of beginning again in their marriage.

CONCLUDING THOUGHTS

Why should you begin to risk an adventure in peer counseling? In the introductory chapter, I pointed out that such mutual sharing and caring were Christ's intention in founding the church. His own example in counseling with persons, the pattern of openness He modeled in his twelve-group, the key phrases He used when He described the church He would build, and the implications of all of His teachings tend to favor the kind of peer counseling among His followers which I have urged in this book.

Furthermore, the very nature of the church as one body as it is taught in the Scriptures favors the sense of belonging, the feeling of being in God's household and family. All of these realities undergird counseling and almost call for peer counseling as a natural expression. You might well ask yourself whether anything else you do with your fellow Christian in the church, such as worshiping, giving, and serving together, is as great an imperative as that you serve one another in peer counseling. It is simply amazing to me that the church has come so far in history without taking its obligation in peer counseling seriously.

Your own experience of the Holy Spirit fruit of long-suffering, goodness, love, joy, and peace will urge you to become active in peer counseling. It is of the essence of the Holy Spirit to be counselor, to be comforter, and to help the unutterable groanings of the human heart to be heard.

Your charismatic gifts of the Spirit will tend to thrust you into peer counseling. You will find the Spirit's gift of "helps" to be just what you need. The Spirit's gift of hospitality will enable you really to open your own heart to your counselee. Your gift of discernment can help you see through the surface issues to the deeper realities. Your Spirit gift of wisdom and knowledge can often make the difference when a "teachable moment" comes, or when you attempt to summarize what you have heard your counselee say. Your spiritual gift of healing may be called forward to help heal hurting memories or sick attitudes.

Your own need to receive peer counseling may get you started. You may risk making yourself vulnerable and go trustingly to a brother or sister in the church for help. You may decide to surrender your isolation and loneliness and begin really to walk out into the light as He is in the light, there confessing your faults one to another, because you deeply believe that it is precisely within that brotherly openness that the scriptural promise is given. It is within that transparent and honest sharing that the blood of Christ cleanses from all sin. If and when you do receive deep and lasting help through counseling, you will feel that it is still more blessed to give than to receive. You will want to comfort others who are in any "affliction" with that same comfort wherewith you yourself have been comforted by God.

Your awareness of needs of your fellow Christians and neighbors may start you in peer counseling. You can't help noticing how persons are seeking one another out to give and receive help in a whole host of peer counseling efforts. Alcoholics Anonymous uses aspects of peer counseling. Divorcees anonymous does so too. Persons suffering from diabetes are meeting to counsel and support one another. There are elements of peer counseling appearing in drug therapy groups. It is being used in college dormitories, among gamblers, weight watchers, and therapy groups.

Sometimes, as the Scriptures note, the children of this world are wiser than the children of light. It is high time for the church to awaken to the potential of peer counseling and to become a leader in its use. Within the spiritual realities which are possible in the fellowship of the church peer counseling can attain a power not possible elsewhere.

In the second chapter I listed nearly twenty happy crises along life's way which may call for members of God's household, the church, to rejoice with those who rejoice. Many of these times of mutual rejoicing will yield tremendous abiding blessings if members counsel with one another about the deeper meanings of the happy event.

I listed next twenty or more painful crises in life which may call for members of God's household to weep with those who weep. Much of this mutual caring and sorrow sharing will be greatly enriched if members offer counseling to the hurting person.

Many of the principles and attitudes which undergird effective counseling apply in any of the forty human crises listed. Many of the skills described in these pages are equally essential whether the problem posed by the counselee is religious doubt, a broken relationship, a vocational choice, a sickness, a temptation to cheat, a decision to marry, a promotion, a terminal illness, a marital problem, or grief over the death of a loved one.

Caring persons who use their common sense as they seek to help one another through life's hard or happy places are already doing one another a tremendous lot of good. It is my hope that this book's ideas may further upgrade the good work caring persons are doing and can do in helping one another.

READINGS AND REFERENCES

Chapter 1
Attitudes and Skills Essential to Counseling

Christenson, Larry. *A Charismatic Approach to Social Action* (Minneapolis: Bethany Fellowship, 1974). Chapter 2, "The Failure of Phariseeism."

Halmos, Paul. *The Faith of the Counselors* (New York: Schocken, 1966). Chapter 3, "The Elements of the Counselor's Faith."

Hulme, William E. *Two Ways of Caring* (Minneapolis: Augsburg Publishing House, 1973). Chapter 5, "The Contemporary Priest and Prophet."

Kemp, Charles. *Physicians of the Soul* (New York: Macmillan, 1947). Chapter 14, "The Changing Emphases in the Cure of Souls."

Oates, Wayne E. *Anxiety in Christian Experience* (Waco: Word Books, 1971). Chapter 9, "Anxiety and the Fellowship of Concern."

Oden, Thomas. *Game Free* (New York: Harper and Row, 1974). Section II, "A Game-Free Relationship."

Viscount, David S. *The Making of a Psychiatrist* (Greenwich: Fawcett World, 1972). Chapter 3, "First Patients, First Encounters."

Chapter 2
Tactful Beginnings of the Counseling Relationship

Anderson, Philip and Phoebe. *The House Church* (New York: Abingdon Press, 1975). Chapter 3, "Building a Faith-Trust Community."

Allen, Tom. *The Face of My Parish* (London: SCM Press, 1966). Chapter 3, "The Place of the Layman."

Brister, C. W. *Pastoral Care in the Church* (New York: Harper & Row, 1964). Chapter 8, "Sharing the Primary Moments of Life."

Fisher, Wallace. *From Tradition to Mission* (New York: Abingdon Press, 1965). Chapter 4, "Dialogue and Encounter."

Klassen, William. *The Forgiving Community* (Philadelphia: Westminster Press, 1966). Chapter 8, "Forgiveness and the Pastoral Task."

Mayeroff, Milton. *On Caring* (New York: Harper & Row Publishers, 1972). Chapter 5, "How Caring May Order and Give Meaning to Life."

Oates, Wayne E. *Protestant Pastoral Counseling* (Philadelphia: Westminster Press, 1962). Chapter 3, "The Holy Spirit as Counselor."

Chapter 3
Skills in Responding and Intervening in Counseling

Benjamin, Alfred. *The Helping Interview* (Boston: Houghton Mifflin, 1969). Chapter 1, "Responses and Leads."

Collins, Gary R. *Effective Counseling* (Carol Stream, Ill.: Creation House, 1972). Chapter 2, "The Course of Counseling."

May, Rollo. *The Art of Counseling* (New York: Abingdon Press, 1965). Part 2, "Practical Steps."

Rogers, Carl R. *Client Centered Therapy* (Boston: Houghton Mifflin, 1951). Chapter 4, "The Process of Therapy."

Sullivan, Harry Stack. *The Psychiatric Interview* (New York:

Norton, 1954). Chapter 6, "The Interview as a Process."

Thornton, Edward E. *Theology and Pastoral Counseling* (Englewood Cliffs, N.J.: Prentice-Hall, 1964). Chapter 2, "Prepare the Way for Salvation."

Yoder, John H. *The Politics of Jesus* (Grand Rapids: Eerdmans, 1972). Chapter 9, "Revolutionary Subordination."

Chapter 4
Vocational Counseling

Collins, Gary. *Effective Counseling* (Carol Stream, Ill.: Creation House, 1972). Chapter 4, "Vocational Counseling."

Oates, Wayne E. *Confessions of a Workaholic* (New York: World Publishing Co., 1971). Entire book.

Schaller, Lyle E., *The Decision Makers* (New York: Abingdon Press, 1974). Chapter 1, "How Decisions Are Made."

Sherrill, Lewis J. *The Struggle of the Soul* (New York: Macmillan, 1953). Chapter 3, "My Father's Business."

Tournier, Paul. *The Whole Person in a Broken World* (New York: Harper & Row, 1964). Chapter 3, "The Rift Between the Spiritual and the Temporal."

Vogt, Virgil. *The Christian's Calling* (Scottdale, Pa.: Herald Press, 1961). Entire booklet.

Zimpels, Lloyd. *Man Against Work* (Grand Rapids: Eerdmans, 1974). Chapter 4, "The economics of Woman's Liberation."

Chapter 5
Premarital Counseling

Clinebell, Charolette H. *Meet Me in the Middle* (New York: Harper & Row, 1973). Chapter 3, "Equal Though Different."

Landis, Judson and Mary G. Landis. *Building a Successful Marriage* (Englewood Cliffs, N.J.: Prentice-Hall, 1962). Chapter 6, "Marriageability."

Morris, J. K. *Premarital Counseling* (Englewood Cliffs, N.J.:

Prentice-Hall, 1960). Section 3, "Methods of Premarital Counseling."

Peterson, James A. *Toward Successful Marriage* (New York: Scribners, 1960). Chapter 4, "Setting the Patterns for Marriage."

Scanzoni, Letha and Nancy Hardesty. *All We're Meant to Be* (Waco: Word Books, 1975). Chapter 9, "Living in Partnership."

Thielicke, Helmut. *The Ethics of Sex* (New York: Harper & Row, 1964). Section 3, "The Order of Marriage."

Chapter 6
Marriage Problem Counseling

Augsburger, David. *Caring Enough to Confront* (Scottdale, Pa.: Herald Press, 1973). Chapter 4, "Getting Unstuck: Experiencing the Freedom to Change."

Clinebell, Charolette H. *Meet Me in the Middle* (New York: Harper & Row, 1973). Chapter 9, "Living with a Liberated Woman."

Gurman, Alan S. and D. G. Rice. *Couples in Conflict* (New York; Jason Aronson, Inc., 1975). Section E. "Facilitating Communication Skills."

Landis, Judson T. and Mary G. Landis, *Building a Successful Marriage* (Englewood Cliffs, N.J.: Prentice-Hall, 1962). Chapter 14, "Achieving Adjustment in Marriage."

Martin, John R. *Divorce and Remarriage* (Scottdale, Pa.: Herald Press, 1974). Part 2, "Counseling Procedures."

Rogers, Carl. *Becoming Partners* (New York: Delacorte Press, 1972). Chapter 9, "Threads of Permanence and Enrichment."

Southard, Samuel, *Like the One You Love* (Philadelphia: Westminster Press, 1974). Chapter 4. "Share Without Surrender."

Paul M. Miller of 1119 South Eighth Street, Goshen, Indiana, is Professor of Practical Theology at Associated Mennonite Biblical Seminaries, Elkhart, Indiana. He teaches courses in pastoral counseling, group leadership and group dynamics, pastoral leadership, and clinical pastoral education.

He holds ThD and ThM degrees from Southern Baptist Theological Seminary, BD and ThB degrees from Goshen Biblical Seminary, and the BA degree from Goshen College.

Reared in Lancaster County, Pennsylvania, he owned and managed a herd of purebred Holstein cattle and operated two farms for eight years. At 31 years of age he began training for a pastoral or missionary ministry.

Miller pastored a congregation for eight years, served as bishop of five congregations for twelve years, researched theological education in East Africa for two years, and served four months in Southern Africa in 1977.

He is author of *The Devil Did Not Make Me Do It* (Herald Press, 1977), *Equipping for Ministry in East Africa* (Central Tanganyika Press/Herald Press, 1969), *Servant of God's Servants* (Herald Press, 1960), and *Group Dynamics in Evangelism* (Herald Press, 1954).

He holds membership in the Association of Clinical Pastoral Education and in the Association of Professional Education for Ministry.

Miller has served as chaplain in three hospitals and as a consultant and facilitator in numerous marriage counseling and couples communication groups, growth institutes, and group dynamic laboratories.

He is married to the former Bertha S. Mumma. They are the parents of four grown children.